ADVANCE PRAISE FOR
THE WINNING MANAGER

"[This book] should be read by all aspiring managers, as well as experienced managers, to get a picture of the real world of commerce and industry. Walter covers a wide spectrum of many practical questions and situations, that academicians generally ignore in their rarefied teaching.

A job seeker who is ready to enter the business world needs to learn the ropes of job hunting, creating value and moving up the ladder of management. The person needs a full understanding of the business challenges and opportunities he or she will face. Those in middle or senior management have other and sometimes more complex challenges, as they move towards the CEO position or towards retirement.

Let Walter be your guide, as you seek to enjoy a rich and rewarding career in management, with his central theme of high performance in tandem with high ethical standards."

–Philip Kotler

Praise for the previous edition

"The author fills his work with many examples and anecdotes to ensure a painless read. (It is) a valuable read to win."

–Business Line

"This is a book of difference. It tears the mask of management theory, which talks mainly about 'what should be', and shows instead 'what it is' that really happens in the workplace. It enables on to learn from other's experiences and not from one's own mistakes.

Walter Vieira uses his enormous experience as a business consultant to present a step-by-step progression of corporate life and to provide lessons for shaping a successful corporate executive. Full of real life examples and anecdotes, this book will enable managers to relate to, and tackle, everyday problems successfully."

–Mid Day

"A guide meant for students of management and those working in the corporate sector, in this book the author uses his experience as a business consultant to present the reality, rather than just theoretical wisdom, pertaining to the corporate workplace"

–The Tribune

THE WINNING MANAGER

THE WINNING MANAGER

Timeless Principles for Corporate Success

Second Edition

Walter Vieira

www.sagepublications.com

Los Angeles • London • New Delhi • Singapore • Washington DC

First published in 1999 as: *Planning for Executive Success*
Published in 2005 as: *The Winning Manager: 51 Steps to Corporate Success*
This edition published in 2014 as: *The Winning Manager: Timeless Principles for Corporate Success, Second Edition*

SAGE Response
B1/I-1 Mohan Cooperative Industrial Area
Mathura Road, New Delhi 110 044, India

SAGE Publications Inc
2455 Teller Road
Thousand Oaks, California 91320, USA

SAGE Publications Ltd
1 Oliver's Yard, 55 City Road
London EC1Y 1SP, United Kingdom

SAGE Publications Asia-Pacific Pte Ltd
3 Church Street
#10-04 Samsung Hub
Singapore 049483

Published by Vivek Mehra for SAGE Publications India Pvt Ltd, typeset in 11/13 Adobe Caslon Pro by Diligent Typesetter, Delhi and printed at The Paper House, New Delhi.

Library of Congress Cataloging-in-Publication Data

Vieira, Walter, 1938–
    The winning manager : timeless principles for corporate success / Walter Vieira. —Second edition.
        pages cm
    Revised edition of the author's The winning manager : 51 steps to corporate success, published in 2005.
    Includes bibliographical references.
    1. Management. 2. Success in business. I. Title.
    HD38.15.V53 2014   658.4'09—dc23   2014   2014009460

ISBN: 978-81-321-1371-3 (PB)

The SAGE Team: Sachin Sharma, Neha Sharma, Anju Saxena and Rajinder Kaur

To
my parents
TJ and Prisca Vieira

*All truly wise thoughts have been thought already thousands of times;
but to make them truly ours, we must think them over again honestly,
till they take root in our personal experience.*

—GOETHE, 1749–1832

Contents

PART THREE
ATTITUDES AND VALUES

FOREWORD

A ncient Indian philosophy broke-down life into various stages or ashrams. These were associated with learning, a productive life as an adult and a family person and then progressing towards service and renunciation. This pattern has continued in some form, with the working, or occupational phase taking centre stage. The educational system is geared towards preparing for a career, but as many executives, both seasoned and fresh would say, it doesn't quite prepare you well enough.

Working life has its many highs and lows driven by achievement and occasionally failure to achieve goals. Early in your career you are more concerned with acquiring and mastering the technical skills in your chosen field and as you progress to middle and senior management it is people skills that come to the fore. But at every stage, right from the beginning, attitude and behaviour help to build and nurture relationships with colleagues, business partners, customers and people you interact with.

As someone who has spent his lifetime working with companies and observing peoples' behaviour, the author has distilled his experiences in an easily understandable form which would be found useful by professionals at all stages of their career. While the options for a career have opened up dramatically in the last few years and continue to evolve as we become a service economy, the basic underpinnings that help you achieve success and win are timeless.

K.V. Kamath
Chairman,
ICICI Bank Ltd.

PREFACE

It was in 1999, that I wrote the first edition of *The Winning Manager* (as *Planning for Executive Success*). In this 15-year period, I have interacted with many, many more companies and managers around the world, and completed 38 years in the field of Management Consulting. And like many others, I have found that the 'more things change, the more they remain the same'. The quote at the beginning of the Introduction to the first edition, therefore, still remains relevant.

It is the same issue of, deciding what you have a passion for?; selecting a company to work for; of managing those above you, around and below you; of ongoing learning to develop human and conceptual skills; of innovating; of communicating and networking; of office politics; of conflicts in values and the high price to be paid for ethics in many corrupt business environments.

I have added chapters which have been some of my columns in the last 10 years and which have relevance to the present context. For the rest, the structure remains the same. As a Marketing Consultant, I am still inclined to treat the executive life cycle, like a product life cycle; rather than following the standard 'management structure' approach.

I hope the new edition will help those on the threshold of a managerial career whether in government or in industry; or those already there—so that they may learn from the experiences of others—and have a chance to experiment and 'tread the paths less trodden'.

Walter Vieira

INTRODUCTION

I was inspired to write this book after reading the following paragraph in an article:

If the universal truths are already known, then why isn't everyone implementing them? Maybe because what isn't discussed are the subtle distinctions, those little nuances that trip us up all the time. Where are those wrong turns located and why do we take them?

I have been a student of management and an observer of managers for nearly 50 years. As a corporate executive for 14 years and a management consultant for 35 years, I have worked with government, public-sector organisations, non-profit organisations, private sector corporations, family-owned and widely-held companies and transnational and local companies. I have interacted with executives at every level—from freshly recruited management trainees, to chairmen and board members. Many of the former were enthusiastic and filled with aspirations and some among the latter, tired and disillusioned.

These experiences and interactions spurred me to cull lessons and write articles, many of which appeared in *BusinessWorld* in a monthly column, for around 20 years.

This is not a standard book on management. It does not attempt to take the reader through the process of planning, forecasting, organising, delegating, motivating, monitoring, controlling and communicating in a sequential order, as in Fayol's *Wheel of Managerial Functions*. Instead, it goes 'beneath the skin' of management, as it were, to discuss issues that are not normally dealt with, either in speech or in writing.

An executive's career path is like a product or corporate life cycle. In the present environment, with globalisation and changes in technology, both have unpredictable time spans.

It begins with the pioneering stage or the start, and continues to the growth stage, then, the maturity stage, and finally, the decline stage and retirement of the executive. In this book, I have dealt with the more important formative and maturity stages. Part of the maturity stage and the decline stage are dealt with in the sequel to this book—'Manager to CEO'.

I hope the reader will enjoy these pieces and that it will stimulate him/her to develop greater insights into occurrences and events to which we generally give little thought, and, like Rudyard Kipling believed, 'to see the world in a grain of sand'.

Walter Vieira

PART ONE

Starting Out

This is the beginning of another chapter in your life: the 'work phase'. We have left the 'learning phase' behind us. And the 'leisure phase' is at least 30 years ahead for most of us. The executive life cycle can be compared to a product life cycle. It includes the starting phase, then growth and last maturity. All these have been dealt within this book.

This is a period of turmoil and change. Tumultuous change caused by globalisation, liberalisation, privatisation and technology, ensure that there are no long-term careers any more, only short-term assignments. Therefore, there is a great need to develop the ability to shift gears and to change career profiles.

The 'learning phase' continues, parallel to the 'work phase', sometimes even through to the 'leisure phase'.

An executive's life cycle is as special and individual as his/her nature. These reflections are signposts which you will come across on the long climb up towards the peak of corporate hierarchy.

1

On the Threshold
Start of the Work Phase of Life

Dream what you dare to dream. Go where you want to go.
Be what you want to be.

—CALVIN COOLIDGE, 1872–1933
30TH US PRESIDENT

The threshold of a corporate executive career is one of the most significant points in your life. It is also perhaps the second time that you have been called upon to make an important and critical decision, the first being the choice of a college course after high school. Often, in developing countries like India, we make neither the first choice, nor the second. The choice of a college course usually depends on the marks obtained and the expected 'earning potential' than on talent and aptitude. Thus, many 'choose' to become consulting physicians when they have the aptitude to become highly creative architects instead; others end up doing routine jobs as accounts clerks in government offices, when they could have been excellent civil engineering draftsmen!

Therefore, when you come to the second big decision—of choosing a 'career path'—it could also be a product more of accident, than of design. The candidate sends out applications in response to every distantly suitable advertisement, looks for leads from friends, relatives and family, and virtually adopts what in selling is called the 'cold canvassing' approach, in an effort to 'sell himself'.

There are two categories of candidates at the opposite ends of the spectrum. There is one category that believes in Doris Day's famous song, 'Que Sera, Sera' (What Will Be, Will Be). They find a job by accident, accept it because they have no choice, stay in it unhappily and finally end up bitter with themselves and with the world.

The other category is the 'outstanding' group—a small one, whose members have many choices. They may be chartered accountants or graduates from top technology or management institutes, or those who perform outstandingly in graduate colleges. Corporate recruiters woo them on campuses. They receive many offers, one better than the other, and get to choose the job and the company—not the other way round. While most in the first category may end up with an unsuitable job without any choice, some in the second category, in an anxiety to grab the highest-paying job, may also end up choosing an unsuitable one. **The 'middle of the road' group may therefore be in a better position (though not necessarily) to take a more balanced decision.**

For many of us in India, therefore, the approach is to make the best of the choices that are available, rather than the best in a 'close-to-ideal' situation. For this, a SWOT analysis can be carried out by the individual. **This exercise helps considerably to focus on how you will live your life, what you will do and the values you will adopt.**

A SWOT analysis is very simple. It is a measurement of (S) strengths and (W)weaknesses, of (O)opportunities and (T) threats. It requires a very honest look at yourself; at your capabilities; at what can be achieved with honest effort and what cannot be achieved at all. It also requires a clear assessment of what opportunities the environment offers and what are the threats and dangers and lack of opportunities in that same environment.

You may have perhaps, consciously or unconsciously, done a SWOT analysis while choosing a course of study at college (marks permitting!). If you were weak at maths and strong in languages, you would have thought about areas that involve qualitative faculties. If you were strong at maths, statistics and physics, you would have become an engineer, physicist or perhaps done soil engineering.

The 'after-the-study' phase is the time for taking stock of yourself again. If you are a professional, i.e. a doctor, lawyer or a solicitor, the path to be followed is different, and well laid out. In this book, we will be talking of the managerial stream in a corporation, in the private or public sector. An engineer, fuel technologist or any other professional can also join the managerial stream. These thoughts would then apply to this group as well.

Now is the time to reassess whether you are a 'loner', a 'member' or a 'leader' of teams. A loner likes to work and achieve alone, and therefore should focus on a career that is individualistic. Others who are gregarious and like to be with people most of the time would be qualified to be members or, leaders of 'teams', enjoying working in a group. Some are 'doers' and, therefore, may like an activity-oriented career; others are 'thinkers' who will therefore prefer a thinking-oriented career. A few others are what are called 'integrators'—who combine a balance of thinking and doing. This is that rare breed who can reach the top. The integrators combine both the faculties and are strong both at conceptual thinking as well as implementing their plans.

Those who have graduated without specialisation have several options—to become creative writers, journalists, film script writers, film-makers or creative personnel in advertising agencies. Others may want to become social workers, or involve themselves in entrepreneur development or rural development. Even for some of these less-trodden paths among careers, there are now specialisation courses, sometimes full-time, generally part-time.

Therefore, **the first thing to do is to discover the kind of person you are, what you would like to do, what you would enjoy doing for the rest of your life.** You may not know yourself totally—but you do have an idea of the kind of person you are and the kind of person you would like to be. You can also assess where you can improve by making up for any weakness, and whether you have the inherent capability to do so.

However, you have to be practical. Does the environment you live in provide the requisite opportunities to make a success of the career you wish to pursue? It could be an area which is already over-saturated and therefore limited in scope. On the other hand, it could be over-saturated, but you are so confident of excelling that you are certain you will do well. Or, it could be an industry where the scope is limited at present, but where there could be a lot of potential in the future, with changes in technology and environment. Or, it may be an industry which is on its way to obsolescence.

Each of us has to scan and assess this environment—looking for the opportunities and the threats. Parents may be able to help, counsel or give general guidance, but finally you have to take your own decision. You are the master of your own destiny. You have to take charge and chart a course. Here is where you begin!

However, you must remember, we are living in a period of tumultuous and rapid change. You cannot plan for a lifetime career and stay with it. You will have to keep changing direction; even changing careers, as you go along. Companies will fail; industries will fail; and new developments will change business history. You will have to keep aligning yourself—like a wind surfer who adjusts direction and speed, based on the wind and the waves. You need to plan as if you will live forever, and live as if you will die tomorrow.

The first step can be the beginning of a long journey.

2

SKETCHING OUT A GRAND CAREER DESIGN
FIXING THE MILESTONES

I hold that man is in the right, who is most closely in league with the future.
—HENRIK IBSEN

Once you have done your SWOT analysis, you are more than half way to knowing the kind of company you would like to work for, the kind of job you would like to do and the kind of career path you would like to follow. Of course, this career path may veer in many directions over the years—some by accident, some due to calculated risks, some to chance encounters. But this does not obviate the necessity to have what may be called 'the grand design'—a plan to start out with. This is necessary, because **if you do not know where you are going, then all roads lead there!**

Now is the time **to look at the location where you may want to work**. It is true that at this stage in life, you cannot be too choosy; you cannot decide to stay put on home base. Most of us are not so lucky, not unless we inherit our father's business! In which case, we may not be required to make any such decisions anyway. But for those of us who do need to make a decision, we may choose to restrict ourselves to the north, the east or the south. This is reasonable, and fair to the corporation and the individual.

I have come across so many sales people who will answer the question in the application form 'Are you prepared to be posted anywhere in India?' with a firm, affirmative, no-nonsense 'Yes'. They are appointed and posted to Dibrugarh or Shillong in the east, or Nasik or Sholapur in the west. One week after the six-month probation period is over and the confirmation of a service letter has been received, the rumblings begin. The syndromes of an only son, old parents, widowed mother, seriously ill sister or sisters to be married suddenly, surface. They all want transfers to the metros. This causes great unhappiness to the individual as well as to the corporation. If the ground rules had been made clear right at the beginning, such unhappiness could have been avoided. The individual must have the courage to stand by the decision taken.

If the decision was taken because of the lack of choices, then you must abide by it regardless. Or change the job and go elsewhere, with another corporation. To stay and whine and complain and fret is only a reflection of a weak-minded but scheming individual who is not valued anywhere else anyway.

Within the geographical zone, **the focus is on the corporation**. What kind of company is it? What kind of reputation does it enjoy? Is it a newly started company or an old reputed one? If new, has it been started by an established organisation or by newly inducted entrepreneurs? If by new entrepreneurs, what is their previous record as individuals? If promoted by an established company, what is their record? Is it a public limited, private limited, partnership or proprietary company? What is the style of management—paternalistic, autocratic, democratic or laissez-faire?

And is it really professionally managed? There are so many proprietary companies which are professionally managed and so many public limited and even multinationals which are managed as if the chief executive's 'grandfather owned the company', that the distinction between professionally and not-professionally managed has become blurred. In the past, people believed that companies managed by paid employees who had no stake or ownership were professionally managed, and those managed by the owners or major shareowners were not professionally managed. This distinction no longer holds true. A strange metamorphosis has taken place and the new entrant has to be all the more careful.

There **are companies with community preferences** and even though they may take on people of different communities on the ground level, the going may become difficult as one climbs up a narrowing pyramid, until community alignment takes place at the senior most level, between the senior management and the 'supremo'.

There **are also education taboos**. Some companies prefer to recruit only MBAs as trainees or junior executives. While some may accept MBAs from any university, others insist on an MBA from one of the premier institutions, such as the Indian Institute of Management, Xavier's Labour Relations Institute, Jamshedpur or Jamnalal Bajaj Institute, Mumbai. If they do accept someone who does not fit this mould, it may be because of an immediate need. But during promotion time, all other things being equal, the MBA will be preferred. This contingency has to be foreseen by non-MBAs, non-CAs in accounts and non-degree holders in engineering; so that one is not disappointed at a later stage in life when it is too late to retrace one's footsteps.

There **are also cultural or style aspects to be considered**. There are companies where an executive without an Oxford accent, or at least a Doon School accent, 'does not belong'. He/she may be good at work, he/she may have the qualification, he/she may be needed and, in fact, be appreciated by the company. But, somehow, because of the background, he/she has to remain on the fringes of the executive social arena, without being an active participant. There are others whose wives do not feel comfortable in what may be termed the 'jet set'. Not for them, the company apartment in upmarket areas of Mumbai like Mount Pleasant Road on Malabar Hill, where the neighbours talk about kitty parties, the latest exhibition of *salwar kameeze*s or paintings at the Jehangir Art Gallery. They may feel much more comfortable in the good, stolid and distant suburb of Mulund in Mumbai where neighbourliness and warm friendliness would generally go together.

There can **be problems of personal beliefs and attitudes**. It is better to sort these out before venturing to send the applications and going through the process of interviews. Is it a company dealing in alcohol and/or cigarettes, products you do not want to be associated with? Are you a vegetarian, applying for a job in a company selling frozen meats? If these things do not matter to you, that's well and good. If they do, it may be better to opt out right at the beginning, than join with reluctance and do a half-hearted job because there is a conflict of beliefs and a divergence of attitudes.

Attitudes can also affect the areas of security, status and family background. There will be those who prefer service in the government, public sector, railways or airlines—because of the security provided, the status the post commands (a status which rarely goes with a private sector job) or because his/her father/grandfather were railway people, or in service, which gives a 'pink tint' to the vision of a career.

All of us have to use some or all of these criteria when deciding to apply to a company. These will help to convert a company from a 'suspect' into a 'prospect'. The candidate does this exercise the same way a company would have done to select a candidate. It may be that at the end of it all, you may choose 'the path less trodden', as Robert Frost would describe it. But since there would be 'miles to go' before you stop, it may be worth taking the time and trouble to do the right thing at the beginning.

3

APPLICATIONS THAT WORK
AND WHY SOME DON'T

Facts do not cease to exist because they are ignored.
—*ALDOUS HUXLEY*

Once you have decided the focus of your attention—in terms of the kind of job you will enjoy, in the kind of company you will like, in a geographical area where you will be comfortable—then you will begin sending out applications and making a bid for the job a company has advertised.

The first step is to keep your eyes and ears open. Buy a range of newspapers and magazines. If you cannot buy them, join a library so you can access the different newspapers and business magazines. You can also contact a reputable placement agency and register with them for suitable job opportunities. Vacancies for trainees are also advertised on the notice boards of leading colleges. There is always the grapevine—and now there is the Internet—a medium that gives you the largest scan at the least cost and with the least effort (naukri.com/linked-in/skillpages/jobs.com and some others).

The second stage is to identify the job you would like to do and then write out an application that shows how you, with your qualifications and experience, fit in the position as described by the company. How do you ensure that your application stands out from the crowd? It takes time and effort to master the art of making your application 'different' and set it apart. The important thing here is that every time you write an application, it must be 'tailored' to fit the requirement. To that extent, just as a Rolls Royce is custom-built, so should be an application. It should not be an assembly-line product. But few people realise this.

A job application should not be handwritten, unless the advertisement specifically says so. Especially if your handwriting is not easily decipherable, it is best to restrict handwriting to just the signature, and have the rest of the matter typed.

A job application should not be an 'obvious' photocopy of an original. This shows that you have been sending applications all over the place, and this is one of the many. You may actually be sending applications all over the place and there is nothing wrong with that. But you don't have to project such an image.

Illegible handwritten applications, photocopies, cyclostyled sheets and faint copies all end up in the wastepaper basket, while you wait and hope for an interview call letter. It is all so easy now with the use of a computer, where each print out is an original.

There are those who use their company letterheads and envelopes to write their applications. This is not acceptable. Using company stationery, and company postage, for personal work is a reflection of a certain laxity in personal integrity. It is not the quantum of money but the principle involved.

Some are so careless and generous with the amount of glue used on the envelope that a part of the application gets stuck and is torn in the process of opening the envelope. Very few in the employer firm will take the trouble to join the torn pieces together. And so, whatever is torn off is missed, and with that, a part of why you should be selected for the assignment.

Use good quality white bond paper to type the application and use matching quality and colour envelope. If you have personal stationery, this is acceptable, even if it is coloured, but not garish. Use an envelope larger than the contents.

Have the application neatly typed, with a layout pleasing to the eye, and without errors. Sometimes applications addressed to me have my name spelled incorrectly. How can an employer call such a careless candidate for an interview?

Use a brief covering letter, not more than one page of your curriculum vitae (CV) or biodata, highlighting your qualifications and experience especially relevant to the job you are applying for. It helps to focus on how your skills match what the employer is looking for, based on his advertisement. It also shows that you have read the ad carefully and given thought both to the employer's needs and to the contribution you can make. It demonstrates that you are not just looking for 'any' job!

The CV attached to the covering letter should be complete in all respects and should have the right sequence, as follows:

(1) Name in full
(2) Address
(3) Telephone number
(4) Date of birth
(5) Marital status
(6) Languages (spoken, read and written)
(7) Educational qualifications
(8) Special assignments
(9) (Details of thesis, project work, any prizes, awards, etc.)
(10) Short courses done, with the period
(11) Professional membership
(12) Employment history (in chronological order, present employment first)
(13) Brief statement of responsibilities and achievements in present job
(14) Hobbies and extracurricular activities
(15) References (at least two)
(16) Salary expectation
(17) Joining date

Some applicants try to skip details, just because these are inconvenient and they feel that disclosure will go against their candidature. So, some don't give their date of birth, because they are older than the age specified; others don't give their qualifications because the ad specified a science graduate, and they graduated in commerce or arts; some do not specify the languages spoken because they do not speak the local language as specified in the ad. This does not help. The applicant feels that he/she will have a chance to clarify and explain at the interview. But he/she may never be called for an interview—and the chance to explain may never come about. It is best to give all the relevant facts, in the right sequence; if necessary, in the covering note. Give an explanation why, despite some disadvantages, you could still be the person who could make a worthwhile contribution.

Many applicants do give all the details, but they keep the name of their present employer a closely guarded secret. They will just say 'large diversified engineering company with a turnover of ₹500 million with headquarters in Delhi'. I have never been able to unravel the rationale for such secrecy. It serves no purpose.

Some applicants are blessed with a large number of well-placed relatives. They plug this fact hard in their CV. They give the name, qualifications and position held by the father, each brother and sister and even the in-laws. The employer is then in a situation where he is more impressed with the great achievements of the relatives than with the mediocre ones of the candidate!

It is a good practice to give the names of two references in the CV. However, the references should be known to the candidate, not just to the candidate's uncle. The references should also be appropriate to the level of the job applied for. It does seem ridiculous to apply for the job of an accounts assistant, and to give the reference of the commander-in-chief of the Indian Army or the governor of a state. Your college professor or former boss, someone who knows you well enough and has some evidence of your performance and ability, are better referees to use. Please always ask the referees for their permission first and only then give their names as references. Later, do keep them informed whether you did or did not get the assignment. These are basic courtesies.

It is also necessary to be clear if you are agreeable to be located anywhere in India, or whether the choices are restricted to a few or even one location. Some candidates imply that they are prepared to be relocated anywhere, but when it comes to the final stage, they insist that they can accept a posting only in a particular city, which can cause a lot of annoyance to the employer.

And what emoluments do you expect? Some write vaguely that their present emoluments are ₹50,000/plus the usual perks. What are the usual perks? Is it a house, a car and chauffeur? It could mean anything or nothing. Once again, instead of helping you by camouflaging the real emoluments, such an approach will only project an image of a person who does not clearly give all the facts.

If care is taken to avoid all these common pitfalls in writing out a job application and to prepare a neat, complete, yet brief document which also explains how the employer will benefit from the skills you have to offer, you would have crossed the first and perhaps the most difficult hurdle in the search of a job—more importantly, the right job for you. In the process, both you and the employer will benefit and find mutual satisfaction.

4

Playing the Interview Game
When Basics Are Often Forgotten

*The worst enemy of human hope is not brute facts, but men of brains
who will not face them.*

—Max Eastman

The interview call. 'Please make it convenient to meet Mr Jal, Personnel Manager, at 2.30 p.m. on 23 January 2010 at the above address.' When you receive an interview call for the first time, or the second, it can send a slight shiver down your spine and make you really nervous. Not to say that an interview call should not stimulate such a response. Many do respond in a manner that gives the event more importance than is necessary. On the other hand, there are some who take the interview call so casually that they seem to be doing the interviewer a great favour by turning up at all!

When a call for an interview is received, **the first thing to do is to pick up the telephone and confirm that you will be attending.** The message is best left with the sender of the call letter or his secretary. Not the telephone operator, as the message may then never be relayed! Alternatively, a written note could be posted or couriered (if it is in another city and the telephone call means a trunk call), confirming your attendance at the interview. Or you can confirm by e-mail. There is the disadvantage here that you may never be completely certain that your message has been received.

It is amazing how many people in India believe that a non-confirmation means that they will, in fact, be attending. They are obliged to respond only if they cannot attend. Something like a wedding reception invitation with the legend at the lower end which says 'RSVP—Regrets only'. But in the case of job interviews, the situation is different. A response is expected, either way.

The second stage is to be clear about where and at what time the interview will be held. If possible, make a check visit to the place a few days earlier if you are in the same town. If you are coming to town specially for the interview, then arrive at least four hours earlier, so that there is enough time to locate the place. I have personally spent a lot of time waiting for people who were an hour late because they went to United India Building instead of Union Bank Building, or to Mafatlal House instead of Mafatlal Centre or to Maker Bhavan instead of Maker Chambers—and all these similar sounding places are a few miles apart. Rushing panting into the interview room an hour late, reflects poorly on the candidate.

The third stage is to be at the interview site at least half an hour before the appointed time. On being sure of the time and place, sufficient time should be left for travel—especially if using public transport. You never quite know how long you will have to wait in the bus queue, or if the scheduled local train is cancelled, or is so overcrowded that you cannot get in, or worse, that you cannot get out at your destination train station. Or the traffic on the road, if you are driving a car arriving in advance gives you time to settle down, compose yourself and wait for the call. Perhaps you can read a brochure on the company kept in the reception area, or a book you have brought along.

You may even need to use the washroom if you have come from a long way or on a particularly squally monsoon day. An early arrival gives you time to freshen up and compose yourself despite the dampening weather.

It may also be a good idea to go through your own application and the standard application form of the company, so that you can refresh your memory about what you have said there. It may seem silly but it is true that what some candidates say at the interview does not tie up with what they have written in the form. Or, they cannot remember dates or have forgotten the names of the referees. All this certainly does not inspire confidence in the interviewer.

What clothes should you wear? This is entirely a matter of personal choice, but it need not look as if the candidate is attending a race event at Ascot, or has taken a break from a family picnic at Manori beach. A sober suit with a sober matching tie, hair in place and well-shone shoes will be appropriate. In short, nothing that will distract from the main focus which is 'you'—and your suitability for the assignment. Loud ties, sideburns, large finger rings, caste marks on the forehead—all tend to distract and, at a subconscious level, affect the interview. There is also a mismatch between a three-piece suit and leather chappals. Although clothes do not make the man, they certainly help to make the interview! It is strange that although advertising agencies and dot.com companies have an informal dress code in their companies, they still expect a certain dress decorum from candidates who appear for a job interview. They may not be as formal as banks or investment firms; but they are also not as informal as they are presumed to be.

There are many other things that go into the making of a successful interview—entering only after a gentle knock; sitting down only after being offered a seat; refraining from smoking, especially if the interviewers are not smoking; refraining from playing with items on the table (ashtray, pen, letter opener); body posture; the tone, at once respectful, yet confident.

Often, interviewees have strange perceptions as to how they should behave. I have seen an old acquaintance, Ravi, enter with an air of 'so you've become big enough to interview me now?'. If he felt strongly enough about this, he should not have come at all! There are others who project an air of defiance, entering with a cigarette dangling carelessly between their lips, clothing as if they have just come in from the beach, speech as if 'I am not really looking for a change, but I just thought I will have a chat and decide'. The endless litany of how every company he/she has worked for, would not have survived without his/her contribution, how well he/she is looked after but is now looking for a bigger challenge, how 'one's' talents are not fully utilised and therefore 'one' (it is not sophisticated to say 'I') is willing to look at something that may be interesting.

Little does such an interviewee realise that interviewers have been through all this before. They have themselves been interviewees. An interview is a serious game. It has to be played to be won and be played by both written and unwritten rules.

5

Negotiating the Interview
Insights into the Minds
of Interviewers

It is much easier to recognise error than to find truth; error is superficial and may be corrected; truth lies hidden in the depths.

—Anonymous

An interview is like a sparring match. You never know what kind of sparring partner you will come across. Therefore, there are two parts to an interview: one is to be prepared for the interview and be self-centred. Do all the right things, which we have discussed in the earlier chapter. The other is to respond in the right manner, to the attitudes, perceptions, behaviour—even foibles—of the interviewer. After all, the interviewer is the customer. And the customer is always right! In a situation like this, you have no choice. You are the salesman, selling your abilities and services. Things would have been different if you were a policeman. It is jocularly said that the policeman is at the other end of the spectrum. In his case, the customer is always wrong!

There will be all kinds of interviewers. There are the 'A1' types who make the candidate feel at home; who have read the biodata in advance; who ask questions and listen; who want to find out how much you know, rather than what you don't know; who are trying to gauge how they can make use of your strengths to fit the available assignment. They are friendly and cordial, and even if you don't get the job, you have the satisfaction that you have made a friend or at least an acquaintance.

There are the 'A2' types, who may not be cordial and friendly, but who follow the principles of good interviewing. They ask questions and listen, and try to find out in an objective way how the candidate will fit the job. You will get fairness and justice out of them, though it is unlikely that you will get any warmth or concern, or the building of even a casual future relationship.

There are the 'B1' types who may be warm and friendly but don't know what good interviewing is. They ask the wrong questions, interrupt the answers, divert the conversation from the objective to something quite irrelevant, and finally, do not know how to take a decision because they have not followed a method or system.

There are the 'B2' interviewers who are cold and clinical, who are not aware of good interviewing techniques. They feel this is their one opportunity to sit in judgement, to show how much they know, rather than find out what the other person knows, to wax eloquent on their own achievements and experiences, rather than find out what the interviewee has achieved. Such interviewers are the most common, and this is a great pity; because then the interviewee has to resort to the subterfuge of ego boosting bordering on flattery, to get the interviewer to 'soften' towards him.

But the 'C' type of interviewers are the worst of the lot. They are the 'gas bags', the 'zero' category of managers who, by some strange quirk of circumstances, have got to where they are. They will sit behind a desk because this is the only source and symbol of their power. Their manner will shame the Spanish Inquisition of medieval times. They will totally reverse God's design of two ears and one tongue, implying a divine error. This is their opportunity to tell a captive audience how great they are, at least within those four walls. And they will have preconceptions—a prejudice against a certain community, against people with large ears or small eyes or short fingers, or against an interviewee whose birth date is not auspicious for the company. Beware of such interviewers; and beware of corporations that harbour such a breed. A career with such corporations can be a trying experience, and you will have no one to blame except yourself. The warning lights had already been flashed during the interview. Despite this, if one chooses to enter, it is at one's own risk.

With the 'A1' types, the response needs to be reciprocally warm, with a clear and complete presentation, by also asking them questions, to clarify your own doubts. With the 'A2' interviewer, your response needs to be cool, not gushing, with a complete presentation and an economy of words. Questions have to be asked respectfully, but asked nevertheless.

With the 'B1' types, the response needs to be warm, but you will need to guide the interview yourself to bring it to a logical conclusion. A brief recapitulation of your biodata will also help because the interviewer is unlikely to be well prepared. The 'B2' interviewer will also need to be guided, but very artfully, so that his ego remains intact. He/she should be given sufficient importance, so strike that delicate balance to show that you know a lot, but just a little less than the interviewer's level of knowledge though this may not exactly be true.

With the 'C' category—beware. It may be better to attend some more interviews and try for another assignment, rather than be left to the mercy of such managers. With the increase in the number of jobs, you may find it possible to 'let this opportunity pass.'

Finally, an interview is a negotiation. And the best negotiation is when both parties have a 'win-win' situation. Each gets what they want. The buyer of services and the seller are not on opposite sides of the table. They are on the same side—to achieve a corporate goal, for their customers, shareholders and employees.

6

Following Up on Interviews
How Far Will You Push?

*A great many people think they are thinking, when they are merely
rearranging their prejudices.*

—*William James*

If you have attended the interview and are really keen on the job,
then it is only natural that you will go through a period of impatience bordering on anxiety. However, most of the time, the company does not share the same sense of urgency. The more impatient
you get, the longer they seem to take.

There is also the question of the investment that you would
have made. Usually, for the first interview, at a junior level, companies expect candidates to attend at their own expense. When
they are called for the second or third interview, then the fares and
board/lodge, if any, are paid. Some large and reputed companies
who are very sure of their screening system and don't rely on a
'hit and miss', will pay the fares even for attendance at the first
interview.

In any case, apart from the investment of money, there would be
the investment of time—leave taken from the existing assignment

for travel and attendance. With the long distances in India, this can extend to two to three days. And the anxiety is only natural.

The communication revolution has brought in many time and money saving conveniences. Many companies now conduct initial interviews on the telephone (long-distance charges are now much lower) and follow-up with video conferencing, where they can see and hear the candidate. Only the final interview may need a personal appearance.

A good way to follow-up on the interview is not to wait till after the interview, but begin the follow-up during the interview itself. It's like playing football—you don't wait for the shadows of the goal post to appear before you think of shooting a goal. You plan it right from the opening whistle. Thus, towards the end of the interview, you can generally assess how the interview went, the level of interest and the warmth generated. It is also likely that you will be asked if you have any questions.

This is the time when, in addition to other clarifications, you can ask when they expect to take a decision on the selection. If told 'by the end of September', repeat this yourself as a reflective confirmation. If it sounds too soon, check out whether they will, in fact, be able to complete the whole selection process so fast. If it seems very long, respectfully find out why it will take so long.

Reconfirm the notice period you have to give to your present employer before you can resign. Explain if you have any leave to your credit. Also, clarify if you are free to join immediately, which should be possible if it is your very first job, unless you want to go on a long enjoyable holiday before you immerse yourself in the next stage of your life—the working phase.

After you have returned from the interview, it is a good idea to send a little note to the interviewer, thanking him for having spared the time (don't say, 'despite your busy schedule,' a meaningless phrase too often used in India) to see you and that you enjoyed the meeting and that you now look forward to hearing from him by end-September with regard to the final decision.

These letters need not be obsequious (unfortunately they often are). They need to be forthright, direct, a reconfirmation of the decision, date expectation and yet respectful.

If you do not hear from the company by the 10th or 15th of October, it is in order to write again, stating that you had attended the interview/s on (dates) _____ at _____ and were expecting the decision to be announced by end-September. Perhaps there has been a delay and you are writing to recheck whether the results have been announced. If you don't hear from the company even after that, forget it. The answer is obviously, 'No.'

During the period of great turmoil—with the meteoric rise and drastic fall in the dot.com era, there were many who were offered assignments at very high salaries, even six months before they finished their MBAs. The situation changed so fast that when students graduated, they were told that revenues had fallen and the offer was no longer valid. Students thus lost six months of exploration time, because they were complacent in the knowledge that they already had an assignment.

They were now regretful that they had not taken good jobs in the brick economy—but had taken on 'high flying assignments' in the click economy, with double the emoluments; only to be left shipwrecked, with no job or income at all!

Most companies do not write regret letters to those who have applied for a position and have been eliminated at the screening stage. Obviously, they do not find it worthwhile to send out thousands of regret letters. Only those who have been selected for an interview hear from the company. This is sometimes announced in the advertisement itself.

Other companies make an announcement in the newspapers, thanking all those who applied for a particular position and informing them that the position has now been filled.

Some companies do not send out regret letters to those who have been rejected at the interview. If they are fair, they will tell candidates at the interview itself that only those shortlisted will hear from the company by a particular date.

I see it another way. If the candidates have spent time and money to attend the interview, it is only fair that the company spends just a little time and money to keep them informed of the progress. In fact, some companies write such beautifully phrased regret letters to the rejected candidates that it really softens the

blow and makes them friends of the company for life. Good interviewing and post-interviewing techniques are an invaluable tool
for effective public relations by the company.

On the other hand, where the candidate is concerned, there is
no surer way of antagonising a company than by making a nuisance of himself by continuing to telephone the interviewer, or
writing follow-up letters every fortnight or sending cables. This is
a sure way to have the door closed on you. Enthusiasm should not
be mistaken for over-keenness, and genuine interest should not be
mistaken for anxiety.

7

CHOOSING AN EMPLOYER
LOOK BEFORE YOU LEAP

It's God's great gift: To do what you like doing best and get someone
to pay you for doing it.
It's when a hobby merges into a job.

—*ANONYMOUS*

If you have successfully mastered the interview skills and lady luck
has smiled on you, it is quite possible that you may land up with
more than one job. Now you have to make the critical decision
to choose the right company. How do you choose the company
you will work for? Part of the decision would have been made at
the time of sending out the application. Some time would have
elapsed since then and you would know more about the company,
than what you knew earlier from hearsay or from what was said in
the job advertisement 'fast-growing professionally managed company' or from the annual report (designed and printed by a large
advertising agency, using many superlatives).

There are many indicators that you can use in taking a final decision on the company to work for. It starts with the receptionist.
What image does she project? How does she handle visitors? Is
her job a chore or an enjoyable occupation? Is the reception room
neat and clean? It need not be stylish or expensive, but it should

have the sparkle and neatness which shows that 'someone cares'. Does the receptionist grumble about the job, the number and kind of visitors she has to handle? Above all, does she smile?

An interesting test is the 'toilet test'—an accurate measure of the concern of any company. Ask to use the toilet even if you don't need to use one. There are many companies where the noxious odours of uncared-for toilets waft right into the reception room. The toilets are wet and dirty, with the flush not working; there are no soap or tissue or towels and the last time a disinfectant was used was perhaps five years ago! There are other companies where the one clean toilet is used by the managing director or the directors, and the key is kept in a private, safe place.

The directors' toilet is the sanctum sanctorum. All others, from the general manager to the watchman at the gate, have to use the general, wet and uncared-for dirty toilet. A 'toilet caste system' has evolved.

There are other companies where the executive toilet is cared for, but the general toilet is not. We had once recruited a female employee for a large construction company in Bombay. She quit after three weeks of joining duty. The company had no toilet for women and the other women who worked there went to an office on another floor and used their ladies toilet surreptitiously. The new employee did not feel comfortable doing this. The company did not seem to care. These matters were too minor for top management. So, she had to fall in line or quit. She quit!

I attended my first interview at Glaxo on a particularly rainy day of June. I was dripping wet, after making the long trip from a Bombay suburb to Worli, and I felt, and perhaps looked like, a wet rag. But one of the pictures etched in my memory is of Ian Mckinnon, then Purchase Director, coming to the door to receive me, taking my raincoat from me to hang it up, turning down the air conditioning and waiting for a hot cup of coffee to be served before he smoothly began what he called 'a very informal chat'. Mckinnon was a director of the company but he built a bridge, used empathy and projected an image for the corporation. A genuine, sincere one. I did not have much to do with Mckinnon after I joined the company. He later became managing director and died some years later. But I always remember him as the one who influenced me to join Glaxo, not by words but by example.

There are many other indicators which show the 'cultural health' of the company. How do employees talk about the management? Is there a general feeling that the management are exploiters, crooks masquerading as gentlemen in grey business suits? How do managers talk about employees? Is there a wide chasm between unionised and non-unionised staff, or between staff and management or between head office and branches? Do they look down with resentment and with the non-verbal feeling that 'you give a little longer rope, and they will be sitting on your head' (a typical Indian expression!). Other questions you can ask yourself are:

How do managers talk about each other? In multiple interviews, many managers give themselves away subconsciously, about how they feel towards some of their colleagues. Are they constantly sword-fighting (like in *Scaramouche*) so that the possibility of their being able to work as a team seems remote?

How do those who have been with the company a long time talk about it? Do they feel that they have been caught in a trap from which they cannot escape? Because no one else will pay them as much or because they are incapable of doing anything else?

What do those who have retired from the company say about it? Do they look back nostalgically? Do they go back sometimes to see old colleagues? Are they invited for the annual get-together? Do they have some friends from the old workplace whose friendship lingers on, even though the corporate bond has been broken?

What do suppliers of goods and services think about the company? Is it fair in its dealings? Or is it the type which never pays a supplier's bill before 120 days (normal) and 180 days (if possible), or uses any excuse, however flimsy, to waive payment altogether?

What is the company's commitment to society and the community? Do they talk a lot about this and do little? Or is it the other way round?

The answers to all these questions will help you to choose the right company and to make the right decision. It is not going to be easy to find the answers, but there is so much at stake in this decision that it is well worth the time and effort.

8

WITHSTANDING PRESSURES
A FORMIDABLE CHALLENGE

One of the 10 rules for success in life, propounded by Cyrus Vance (author of Manager today, Executive tomorrow), is 'progress means different things to different people'. Do not use the achievements of others, to measure your own success. Each of us **need to set our own goals, based on our capacity and capability**. And then we have to measure ourselves against these goals. Each one is called to play a different role. If we play this well to the best of our ability, **we would not just be happy but contented**; doing what **we like to** do, rather than doing what **we have to** do.

I was, therefore, distressed to read a headline in the *Times of India*, 11 December 2012, *IITians struggle to live up to families fat package dreams*.[1] A student of civil engineering confesses that four years ago, when he qualified in the JEE, his family members were thrilled and shared their joy that he would soon be earning in dollars. **The pressure to live by their expectations, is constantly weighing on him**. It would seem that, enough is never enough!

Another student who had just cleared the JEE, wanted to do aeronautical engineering. But his ambitious and enthusiastic father did a quick survey of all the IIT departments, and was put

---

[1] *The Times of India*. 2012. 'IITians Struggle To Live Up To Families Fat Package Dreams', *The Times of India*, New Delhi, 11 December.

off by the average salaries offered to past students of aeronautical engineering (poor compared to other departments). So, he pushed his son into doing electrical engineering. Who knows? **We might have lost an outstanding aeronautical engineer for an average electrical engineer!**

There are many presumptions that mislead parents and students.

(1) that every IITian gets multiple offers, and is spoilt for choice
(2) that every IITian gets a choice of rupee and dollar salaries
(3) that every IITian has a choice of working abroad
(4) that only technical skills and exam performance will bag them the best jobs
(5) that the highest salary (got by one or two) of ₹60/80 lakhs pa is the average salary offered

None of the above are true. It is only a few that may have the options. The others have to accept local jobs at ₹8/11 lakhs pa and be happy that they are gainfully employed.

Unfortunately, the setting of wrong and unrealistic goalposts, does not end with the first placement. A vice-president of one of the large companies of a conglomerate in India, applied for the position of president of a mid-sized company. I asked him why he wanted to change. He was happy in his job; had climbed the ladder steadily over 20 years; was not unhappy with his company or the boss; was paid adequately by market standards. The answer: **most of my batchmates from the class of 85 have become presidents**. I am still a vice-president. I convinced him to stay where he was, and use his own measure of progress. He stayed, to later become the president of the large conglomerate!

Progress means different things to different people. But if you do something useful; make a contribution and have passion for what you do you will achieve 'contentment'—which money alone can never buy!

9

KNOWING THE CEO
THE CEO CASTS A SHADOW

*The people who think it a shame when anything goes wrong, who rush
to the conclusion that the evil could or ought to have been prevented
are those who, in the long run, do most to make the world better.*
—JOHN STUART MILL

Why should someone joining at the lowest rung bother to
know anything about the chief executive officer (CEO) of
the company? How does it matter to him/her? Why should he/she
spend time and effort to find out the lore about the CEO of the
company he/she intends to join?

A young man recently turned down a good offer because he
found out that the CEO had gone to Patna by air to inaugurate
the company's new depot for Bihar. And he had his Mercedes
driven down from and back to Mumbai by his driver for his use
for three days! Such extravagance, when he could so easily have
hired even a luxury car locally in Patna! This action demonstrated
the CEO's misguided sense of values. The balanced young man
did not care for such a vulgar display of wealth. He did not join
this multinational company, but accepted another assignment at
a lower salary.

Another CEO is known to call divisional heads to individual review meetings to the head office from other factory or office locations within the same city and then keep them waiting for three or four hours before calling each one in. This is such a waste of the time of highly paid managers, while at the same time demotivating them and lowering their self-esteem.

One CEO of a large, listed company is known to privately own a chemicals unit, which supplies the total production to the company. It is widely known that sometimes the supplies have failed on quality standards, but the CEO has insisted that the supply be accepted.

There is yet another CEO who was known to appoint all his relatives and friends as stockists for the company. Many of them did not know anything about the product and have no distribution experience. Since the product had a semi-monopoly for many years, it did not matter too much. But with the changed market environment and increased competition, the cracks began to show. The CEO's system of stockist appointment was then totally exposed for all to see.

There are CEOs who have no other interests beside the job. No golf, no bridge, no other games or hobbies, not even the annual holiday, lest the corporation crumble in their absence. One has to beware of such CEOs. They are generally inclined to be intolerant and narrow-minded—single-track, small-vision men who are good material as corporate cogs. Perhaps they help to increase the share value for the shareholder, but are poor material as society or community catalysts despite their powerful positions.

At the other extreme, there may be CEOs who are interested in everything but their jobs. They have somehow arrived there by a combination of luck, good connections, old school tie, bootlicking and bean spilling. They believe that the application of the same techniques will keep them in the saddle. In many of these cases, the damage done by sins of omission is gradual and unobserved, except by a trained eye. But after a few years, well after the CEO has retired and gone away, the company finds it has retrogressed so far that it will require an exceptional CEO to now make amends.

There is also the CEO who likes to be surrounded by sycophants. He/she wants his/her bags to be carried by his/her vice-presidents at the airport. He/she expects to be checked-in by a standby. He/she arrives with a flourish just as the last passenger has finished with security.

There are stories of extravagance, of corruption, of unethical behaviour, of favouritism and other misdemeanours. And in every company, CEO stories will waft around like Tennyson's 'It looks as if a box of essences was broken in the air'. They could be good exemplary stories or the reverse.

The obvious question is: 'Why should it matter?' Because, for better or for worse, the CEO casts a shadow across the whole organisation. His/her character, personality, beliefs, values and even opinions, superimpose on a corporation and colour it. Employees who may never meet the CEO, who may be many levels below him/her in the corporate hierarchy and perhaps working thousands of kilometres away from the headquarter, are still influenced by his personality.

As a young entrant you should examine all this. This is the final door you have to open to your working career. You have already chosen the industry that you will work in, because it ties in with your speciality or your aptitude, or because it is a growth industry. You have sometimes chosen the location. Now you have to choose the company.

It is not easy to do this. Mercifully, or not so mercifully, in India, many new entrants do not have the opportunity to choose. They are grateful for the job they get. The first one, the only one, is the best one. But there are others—from the Indian Institute of Technology, the Indian Institute of Management and those who return after studies abroad—who have a choice. And they have to take care to choose well.

Again, fortunately for them, there will be many more exemplary CEOs than the 'others'. These 'others' have been described in some detail so that they are quickly identified and as quickly avoided. So the alternatives can still be many.

All this may appear quite complex and time-consuming. It may sound like a market research project. And it is. But does it mean that a candidate will find a perfectly suitable job with a company? Very unlikely. All of life has imperfections, and this area of life will also have its fair share.

Some will offer less money, but greater challenge and higher job satisfaction. Others will offer more money, but a more restrictive environment and a stodgy hierarchy. There will be some who offer a steady career, gradual progress and an enviable company image.

The bigger challenge will be to identify companies like Enron in the USA, and Good Value Investments in India, who present an attractive appearance, on the outside, but are guilty of 'gross corporate misgovernance' on the inside. You often find that these companies are able to camouflage their 'real profile' for a long time, before they are unmasked by someone with a conscience 'blowing the whistle'.

The key is to keep your eyes open to both the plus and minus of the industry, the company, the career and the job situation. It should not be like a blind man walking into a dark room looking for a black cat which is not there!

10

THE FIRST JOB CHANGE
A MAJOR HURDLE

*I never dared to be a radical when young for fear it would make
me conservative when old.*

—ROBERT FROST

So you settle down in the company of your choice. All seem to go well for a few years. It could be three years or six—and then somehow you feel that you are just not making any progress. You have become part of the scenery and are taken for granted. You are making a good and honest contribution to the company, and perhaps in a critically important slot. But when it comes to the annual increment, or promotion, then you are given the 'regular' increment or bypassed for promotion. 'Raj is always with us, has been and will be', is the attitude of top management towards you. So, what do you do? Look for a change of job. This is a crisis that many young men and women come up against. They would have joined fresh out of college, either engineers, MBAs or chartered accountants. They might have been recruited on campus, and been impressed by the presentations made by the company on its track record and its vision of the future. Or they might have applied to the company and got selected after a series of rigorous interviews.

The first job change is a critical one. It is a change which will determine the future progress of the individual. A wrong move at this critical juncture can mar one's career path and change the direction.

To make sure that you do not make a mistake at this point, you will have to take a few precautions.

(1) Check if your present judgement of your first company is the same as when you joined it. If you now find it different (from the 'inside') from what you had perceived it to be when you decided to join, it makes your change much easier. But if the company is true to its projected image, then you have to think about the change very carefully.

(2) Ensure that you have spent a sufficient number of years in your first company. This is fair to yourself and to the company. This period will have given you time to do some learning right from the basics, and then also time to make some contribution to the company which has invested in you. There is no absolute timeframe. The period can vary from three to five years at the minimum, to seven to ten years at the maximum.

(3) Make a proper and objective extrapolation of your career within the company. You may make slower progress here, but reach much further in the long run and be much happier in an environment where you have been trained and nurtured. A new company making an attractive proposition to you may give you an immediate big jump, but in the long run, you may hit a plateau much earlier and finally reach a dead end.

(4) Make sure that you will gain substantially in financial and 'responsibility' terms. Vague promises of future prospects may never be converted to reality. There must be immediate gains. If you are to wait and gain, then you may as well wait in your existing company. The company may be employing you only because they can't get someone who may be more suitable, but will be far more expensive. And they

cannot afford it just now. But when the company grows in a few years, they will, in fact, start filling in the slots from outside rather than promoting the people from below.

(5) Don't be carried away by big designations. Smaller companies use the ploy of giving high-sounding designations to attract young and ambitious talent. Being called 'Assistant Vice-President Operations' of a ₹5 million turnover company means very little and will not fool anyone in the commercial world. At best, it may fool some of the people (your friends and relatives) some of the time, and this is of little use to you, either as a present or future investment.

(6) Don't think that the route—of a junior job in a large company to a senior job in a smaller company to a senior job in a large company—will always work. It may not. If you move to too small a company, or to a 'slow growth' company, you may just get stuck. You will remain a small-company man for the rest of your career, and get 'typed'. You will have to weigh the pros and cons very carefully, before you take a final decision.

If you have considered all these factors, and still want to make a change, then you should. Perhaps you may even want to change your skills/function, together with the change in company. You will then have taken an important step—a milestone in your executive career.

The first change is always the most difficult. It is the first time you have to reorient yourself. It is the first time you have to readjust to a new environment. The future in the new company always seems uncertain. It's like being in the driver's seat alone, after the driving lessons are over. It's like diving into the swimming pool the first time. It's like going out of the country the first time. It will never be the same again. Even if you make six other job changes later in life, it will never be like the first time.

So you have to be sure that you are moving forward in the right direction. And that you will never regret taking the action that you did.

11

BE WARY OF TITLES
THEY CAN BE MISLEADING

*A purchased slave has but one master; an ambitious man must be a slave
to all who may conduce to his aggrandisement.*

—JEAN DE LA BRUYERE

When changing jobs, you should not end up in a situation
that is worse than your current one. The new company may
give you more money and a grander designation. But does it mean
more responsibility? The executive today has to be doubly careful
about designations. The whole area of executive designations has
changed considerably over the last 20 years. In the past, organisations were small and organisation structures simple. You joined
a company at the lowest level: perhaps as accounts clerk or salesman or management trainee. You graduated in time to become a
junior officer/executive/manager, then to senior officer/executive/
manager. And if you were lucky, then you became the general
manager or the managing director.

The environment has now changed and become very compli-
cated. Organisations are now large, multilocational, multiprod-
uct, with diverse interests. And designations have followed suit
and also become very complex. Even at the level of salesmen,

changes took place when salesmen in some industries began forming unions and claimed the classification of 'workmen'. Some companies, where salesmen were highly paid, redesignated them as sales officers or marketing officers, sales promotion officers or sales communicators. The term 'officer' did not mean that one had reached the next level of supervising the work of other salesmen. Only the nomenclature had changed, but the job content remained the same as before.

And in turn, sales supervisors became area managers/area field managers; some were even called business development managers or, worse, regional sales managers. In the past, the sales supervisor looked after a state or a part of it and reported to a regional sales manager who looked after a region, a quarter of a country (north or south, east or west). In the process of recruiting an all-India sales manager, where we needed to consider candidates who have had experience in an entire region, I erred by calling some sales supervisors for interviews, because they had indicated their designations as regional manager. Errors like this mean a waste of a lot of time and money, and can be very frustrating.

When the government introduced a ceiling on the remuneration of directors, there began an exodus from the board room. The managing director resigned from the board, and became the president. The other directors became vice-presidents either in the area of marketing, finance, personnel or production. Later, when the ceiling was considerably raised, some presidents reverted to managing directors, others did not. And now you have a mixture of directors and vice-presidents in corporations around the country.

In the meantime, some other companies began appointing directors who were called directors, but were not on the board of directors. Thus, there was a marketing director, who was head of marketing and whose job function was the same as that of marketing manager. Only the title had changed. Since a large number of directors were thus appointed, there was a need to distinguish between executive directors, who worked full-time in the company and were also on the board of directors; non-executive directors, who were on the board but were not in the full-time employ of the company and directors, who were full-time executives, but not on the board of directors.

The chairman of the board of directors was also having problems. Some chairmen wanted to continue being chairmen beyond their retirement age. If they had done yeoman service for the company, the company reciprocated by designating them chairman-emeritus, something like a field marshal in the army: not quite active, but to be called upon in the event of an emergency. In any case, it was a recognition of significant contributions made. And for a chairman of a large corporation, who has a large team of effective and high-flying executives at the next level, all wanting to be chairman as early as possible, there is the option of creating positions of vice chairman and then again, at level lower, deputy chairman. Another two tiers between the chairman and the other directors on the board!

Years ago, general managers were just that. They looked after the total enterprise and all functions reported to them. Over a period of time, the general manager has become a grade, not a job function. And so, when a person is introduced as a general manager of a company, you now have to take care to clarify whether he/she is general manager marketing, production or personnel. He/she may be in the general manager grade, and looking after a particular function. He/she may even be doing this particular function in a particular division of the company, and not for the total company. So he/she may be general manager (personnel), dyes division. Surely such a long designation can cause confusion in environments not familiar with these developments!

There are also controllers—a term perhaps derived from aircrafts and airports, with titles like navigation controllers. Companies may have a grade of finance controllers and marketing controllers, and the level this implies is as high as the director, or as low as the storekeeper, depending on the whim of the company. Once again, when introducing a controller, one has to be very clear in order to avoid confusion.

There are also senior vice presidents, senior general managers or senior controllers.

Some companies also went to the other extreme. A large pharmaceutical company in India decided to eliminate all executive designations—except the managing director. Visiting cards just said 'A.K. Roy—Marketing Department', whether he was product manager or marketing manager. The company thought it would do away with the 'caste system' derived from titles. Over a period of the next two years, 60 per cent of executives left the company.

Now we have the large Sahara Pariwar which also de-emphasises titles and calls its managing director—the chief worker, and all others at different executive levels are just 'workers.'

Nomenclatures and titles are becoming very important in India. They give prestige and self-assurance. And therefore, there is a scramble for a title which is not always totally appropriate, and sometimes quite confusing. But you have to be careful. Is the new designation being offered to you by your existing company, or by another company trying to attract you; is it only of cosmetic value, or is it substantive? This will take some intelligent exploring, so that you can take the right decision in the overall interests of your own career.

12

UNDERSTANDING LONG-TERM GAINS
LOOK BEYOND THE HORIZON

Do you look for short-term gains? Or do you look at the long-term? In some ways, investing in a career is like investing in stocks. There are some stocks that you buy today—sell within three months; make some profit (occasionally a loss); pay higher tax on short-term gains; and move on—to the other stocks! There are others where you buy, because the fundamentals are very strong; the future market is very large—and your stocks value could increase 10 times in five years; and you pay no tax on capital gains!

There are some who invest in long-term career gains. Those who are not tempted by the 'here and now'. Who are prepared to wait! As they say, when an American goes to a negotiation he goes as a hunter. Aim and shoot. If he succeeds, that's good. If he doesn't, he packs his bags and returns home. The Japanese goes to a negotiation like a farmer. He plants the seed. He nurtures it. He waits for it to grow. He is patient! He has a long-term view and he succeeds!

Anand did a degree in electronics engineering and then an MBA. At campus interviews he was selected by a Finance Investment company in the commercial capital of Mumbai; on a good five-figure pay package. He worked here for two years. He did well—performed up to expectations and earned a bonus both years. And then, he did the unexpected. He resigned. He sought a job in a large IT company in Bangalore. He was offered 60 per cent of what he earned in the finance company. He joined Wipro to everyone's surprise. His parents of course, were distraught. Why should Anand do a thing like this? Is he out of his mind?

When I talked to Anand, what he said made sense to me. He was tired of doing the same thing everyday for two years. He was not learning. His experience was going to be of one year—multiplied by five. Not the experience of five years. He saw the boundaries constantly expanding in IT companies. He could keep learning—always something new. He wanted to be at the frontiers of knowledge; in a knowledge economy. And for this, he had to pay a price. The lower emoluments. He was making a loss now—to gain much more later!

Fifteen years ago, I was hired to select the head of IT services for a large, multinational bank. They were just starting up their IT division in a big way. We advertised the job and received a large number of applications. After screening; and then interviews, we selected Rahul, a senior manager from the largest IT company in India. My client offered him a 100 per cent increase in emoluments. He could now get a company flat in midtown, compared to the present one in the distant suburbs. He would get a chauffer-driven car, when now he had only a conveyance allowance. Besides all these allowances, there would be a substantial increase in salary. We were all happy—my client, the candidate and me!

Imagine my shock when four days later, Rahul turned down our offer. 'Why?' I asked him on the phone 'What is the shortfall? Do you need a further increase? I thought we had been more than fair to you.'

'I am sorry Mr Vieira' he replied. 'It is really not your fault. You have been fair and more than fair. It is just that in my present company, I am continuously being trained. Every four months we have a training programme. I am always at the frontier of technology. In software, this is important. What was current five-years ago, is no longer relevant.'

Now if I join this bank, I will spend two years setting up all the systems and ensuring everything goes smoothly. And when it does? What? After two years, what I knew and what I know, will be irrelevant in IT terms. I would have gained for two years to be outdated in my field for life!

Today Rahul is a vice-president of the software company. His knowledge is relevant. His emoluments are now quite high. And Rahul is happy!

He paid the price to forego short-term gains—for long-term advantages. This requires clear thinking, definitive goals and a sense of discipline. It distinguishes the men from the boys!

PART TWO

Developing Skills and Abilities

There is never an end to developing skills and abilities. Learning is a constant journey without a final destination.

Most of us have become even more acutely aware of the need for 'ongoing development' with the advent of the information age! It has made us seem illiterate—and forced us to virtually 'begin again' and 'yet again'.

13

GETTING ON WITH YOUR BOSS
AN ONGOING CHALLENGE

The boss said: 'You are like a son to me. Disobedient, insolent and rebellious.'
—ANONYMOUS

Whether it is your first job, or a new job, you will be spending a lot of time with your boss. Your boss can make or mar your career. Therefore, getting on with the boss is a very important aspect of an executive's career. Every boss wants to feel like a boss, be treated like one, and if possible, be respected as one. For a salesman, the customer is the 'star'. For an employee, the boss should similarly be made to feel like a star.

But sometimes there is a mismatch. The subordinate could be much better qualified and more knowledgeable and effective than the boss, and very obviously so. The contrast would strike any observer. In such cases, the subordinate had better find another assignment where such a chasm does not exist. This explains why, in many companies, the standards of leadership keep falling with every decade. Mediocre bosses recruit less-than-mediocre subordinates, who in turn carry on the tradition—until finally, the levels fall abysmally low. As does the company.

There is the story of a young executive who wanted to meet the boss to get some papers signed. The matter was urgent, but every time he peeped into the boss's room, there were two ladies present. When at last he managed to meet the boss and explain that he could not enter the room earlier because of the visitors, the boss waved grandly and said, 'Well, you could have come in. It was just my wife and Elizabeth Taylor'. 'And which one was your wife?' asked the young man. Surprised and pleased, the boss dug his hands into his pocket, brought out a $10 note and pressed it into the young man's hand. 'James, son', he said, 'when you become president of this company, remember that I gave you a loan of $10 today'. Such is the refinement of the technique of making the boss a 'star'!

Getting on with the boss is an art. It must have style. It cannot be obvious. It need not be ingratiating. Many executives resort to unsavoury flattery. They laugh loudest at the boss's silliest joke. They carry his/her bag and sometimes his/her jacket as well, at airports. They offer to buy vegetables from the market for the boss's wife. It can be sickening for all those around, and even repulsive to an astute boss who has some modicum of dignity and self-respect.

The boss needs support. He/she needs to be seen as the leader of a group of loyal men. He/she needs support at meetings and at conferences, and especially when he/she is not present. If you speak well and respectfully about him when he/she is not around, he/she will appreciate it more. Don't worry, he/she will get to hear about it.

The boss needs additional information. Not just on what he/she has asked for. Not just a literal following of instructions. There are a lot of things he/she may not know, especially in this age of information explosion. If you take the trouble to go beyond the brief and try and get more information to help him make better decisions, he/she will indeed be appreciative.

The boss needs correction. He/she will certainly be grateful for help in not making mistakes. Or, being made to realise a mistake as soon as it has been made. And he/she will be grateful if the correction is done in private, and in a style and manner where it projects genuine help rather than an 'I-know-better-than-you-do' attitude.

The boss needs projection as a leader. When you have made some significant contribution, developed a new idea, negotiated a big order, or whatever, give credit to the boss. He/she will know that he/she did nothing or little, and that you still publicly gave him the credit. Unless he/she is one of those (and there are some) mean-minded guys, most bosses will remember your generosity and compensate you adequately at some point.

The boss wants patience. He/she does not want young James to be in a hurry to grab his/her chair. It could give him a sense of insecurity; he/she could feel uncomfortable and the bridge of understanding could be irreparably broken. Nothing is as sacred to the boss as the maintenance of his/her own position. And the more average he/she is, the more sacred this mission.

The boss wants you on his/her side. In any company there will be groups or camps. It is possible that your boss belongs to one. It is also possible that this camp is in conflict with another camp, either overtly or covertly. He/she will not want you to be a friend of the enemy. At best, he/she will not mind a neutral stance— neither friend nor foe. And it is best that you keep it that way. You never know when in future a member of an opposing camp may be your next boss.

The boss needs a listener. They are so rarely found these days. Everyone is a talker. Few are the listening types. If there are troubled days, with periods of stress and tension, he/she needs to talk to someone who is also in the know and understands.

And yet, a word of caution. **Loyalty to the boss cannot be absolute. It cannot be blind. It cannot be totally irrational.**

Any intelligent person will not be able to suffer a fool of a boss for long. The primary loyalty is always to the assignment—for which you are compensated, with a secondary loyalty to the company and then to the boss, in that order.

Now times have changed. **In the knowledge economy, many times the position of 'boss' is not permanent.** Software development companies work on a matrix organisation. Hierarchical levels are virtually absent. Teams form, plan, execute and complete a project and disband. Another team is then formed for another project. The team leader in the project for banks, may become a team member in the next project for insurance. The selection of team leader is based on his/her knowledge and experience, in that 'particular' field. A team member in the first team may become a team leader in the second team and therefore roles are reversed. The position of 'boss' is transient and need based. And because of this, it generally ensures greater fairness and better interpersonal relations than in the semi-permanent hierarchical structures of the manufacturing age.

Some Secrets You Should Not Reveal to Your Boss

(1) That you are smarter than him/her
   To imply this through verbal, written or non-verbal com-munication in private, or worse, in public, can be your undoing.
(2) That you know his/her weaknesses
   By all means, cover-up for your boss, but do it subtly, so that he/she feels that he/she did it himself.
(3) That you know about his/her indiscretions
   Whether it is about his/her love life, or mildly corrupt practices, stay mum.
(4) That you know about his/her past
   Especially if he/she was sacked from the previous assign-ment, or relegated to a position of no importance for inef-ficiency, there is no reason to bring those issues up.
(5) That you are looking for other/better opportunities else-where
   You may be seeking other opportunities to learn and to improve, and perhaps also for more money, but it would be indiscreet to tell your employer that you are doing so.
(6) That you are being underutilised, considering your level of efficiency
   If you do this, you will find much of the work of the de-partment dumped on you.
(7) That your passion for your hobby is perhaps more than for your job

Provided that your passion does not take up any of your work time; there is no need to feel guilty about it and for your boss to get involved in it.

(8) That your children are doing better in school than his/her children

By doing this, you increase the tier levels of competition between the two of you, and at senior levels, this can be an additional irritant.

(9) That your spouse is very wealthy

This would imply that perhaps you can do without a job in this company, and at this salary!

14

A Mentor Can Help You Succeed
Makes the Journey Easier

The best way to get ahead in life is to help others get ahead.
—*Anonymous*

We often hear a comment—'However did he get so far? He seems to be such a fool!' And the quick response: 'He's lucky to have a godfather somewhere!' This is such a commonly heard comment in corporations round the world. So it's not exceptional to have a mentor. In fact, it may be rare to succeed without having one. Most times, a young person on the executive career path needs to have a mentor, someone who will take him under his umbrella—who will have a feeling of kinship; who will give the corporate equivalent of paternal care.

The executive cub either selects a mentor; or the mentor selects the cub. It can work either way. Although generally, it may be the latter. This can occur on a 'one-to-one' relationship or on a 'one-to-some' relationship. The mentor–cub relationship can occur for various reasons—the mentor wants an aide or a following; wants to show gratitude for loyalty, to show partiality to someone from his/her family or community or perhaps he/she is just looking for a prospective son-in-law!

In Glaxo, India, the first batch of two management trainees was under the special charge of the Finance Director Mr Gandhi. In most companies, such trainees work under the aegis of the personnel department. But not in Glaxo. Perhaps, it was due to the fact that Gandhi had mooted the plan for such induction. Or, he/she had a special interest in grooming trainees. Since the number of inductees was only two or three in a year; Gandhi became the mentor for the trainees. Whether the trainee was positioned in sales, personnel or purchase, he kept in regular touch and they indirectly reported to Gandhi. It was a purely professional mentor–cub relationship on a 'one-to-some' basis.

In another company, the bright, young, result-oriented marketing manager, Roy, was promoted and transferred (from India) to Jakarta for five years as general manager for Indonesia. He had many strong qualities; and some noticeable weaknesses. One of these was that he had strong likes and dislikes. And he would do anything for those he liked. All he asked of them was undivided loyalty. And when this big break came to the 35-year-old stud from the executive stables, Roy could not resist the temptation to reward those who had accepted him as undisputed leader. And so, he became a mentor; 'one-to-some.' He goaded the management to allow him to take to Indonesia, a sales promotion manager, a marketing services manager and a design artist from the marketing department in India. The staff in Indonesia were not as enthusiastic about this move, as the team of three were. The influx was resented. Over a period of a year, the level of cooperation of the local staff dipped so low that the general manager had to be replaced. And the cubs had to go with the mentor. The 'one-to-some' relationship based on favouritism did not work and finally did damage to both the mentor and those who sought shelter under his umbrella.

There was a managing director, Rob, seeped in the customs of his people, with a very special soft corner for them in his heart. Even in cosmopolitan Mumbai he remained essentially parochial. So when he had a vacancy for a marketing manager and he advertised, he identified and selected a person who was least suited to the assignment—a masters in statistics, who worked in a market research company—with no marketing experience! But he came from Rob's part of the country! He was a kinsman, and against his better judgement and the judgement of others whom he generally consulted—he went ahead with the appointment. For the next five years, Tom became Rob's alter ego. Rob was the mentor— Tom the cub. Tom could do no wrong. He was the son that Rob never had, but wanted. Tom made rapid progress up the executive path—a one-to-one 'mentor to cub' relationship, which was unprofessional and did considerable damage to the general morale among all other company executives.

Or it may have nothing to do with kinsmanship based on the same part of the country. It could just be old loyalties. When Sam was the general manager of a large pesticides firm, he had nurtured Jan as his cub. He had begun as an executive assistant and over seven years moved into the grade of deputy general manager. When Sam resigned to become managing director of a large firm, he took Jan soon after, as general manager of one of the new company's subsidiaries. Some years later, when Sam became chairman of the company; Jan moved in smoothly as his successor; many other senior and perhaps more deserving claimants, notwithstanding!

Very few can really succeed right to the top, without a mentor. Doing it alone, is doubly difficult. It becomes a daunting and formidable task. However, the brilliance of the cub is to ensure that he/she hitches his/her wagon to the right star—the star that is shooting upwards and forwards. That he/she chooses a star who will not perceive him/her as a threat to the star himself. Such a hitch should not cause problems with one's own immediate boss with a conflict of interest and objectives. It is important that the tie-up is not so evident and die cast that with the mentor leaving the corporation, the cub will be left bereft and bereaved. The cub should be able to go on. Finally, the cub should get the mentor to 'want to take him/her under his/her umbrella, because he/she can also be useful to the mentor'. And it is best that the mentor–cub relationship is based on a foundation of mutual professional benefits than any other consideration of family, community and old school tie. This is an ideal situation.

After taking all these factors into account you just have to go ahead with finding a mentor without worrying too much about what may go wrong.

15

Don't Let Accidents Derail You
They Can Be Opportunities
in Disguise

Trying times need not drag you down, if you will see them as doorways
to new beginnings

—Anonymous

On a visit to Mauritius some years ago, I met the scion of one of the largest business houses in the country. It is the house of Currimjee, who deal in a wide range of products from computers to cars. They have been in Mauritius for nearly a century—and I was curious to know how grandpa Currimjee came to this country a 100 years ago—right across the ocean from Kutch in India. The grandson told me that his grandfather was on his way to East Africa. The ship he was travelling on developed some engine trouble. They pulled into Port Louis at Mauritius to have the problem fixed. The young 18-year-old Currimjee who had walked out of the house after an argument with his father, to seek his own fortune, liked what he saw. He assessed that there could be tremendous potential for trading in Mauritius. He set up shop—and began as a small trader. He built this into a large empire, which his sons and grandsons have expanded on. **An accident had proved to be a turning point.**

Dr Krishnaswamy was the Glaxo medical representative with headquarters in a town in south India. He was an effective medical detailer—although why as a doctor, he became a medical representative is something I could never discover. In his mid-forties, Dr Krishnaswamy developed blindness. He could not move around anymore, as he did earlier. The company gave him a desk job at the Madras office. He started out as a sales administration assistant and moved up rapidly to become the branch sales promotion manager. He seemed to blossom in his new assignment. With the loss of his eyesight, his other senses became more sensitive. He could recognise a person by the fall of a footstep. He would address you by name, when you knocked at the door and entered. When I once went to see him, he requested me to please sit till he finished dictating a few letters. He dictated five replies and wound up to attend to me. Later, I discovered that 'doctor' as he was fondly called—had his secretary read out 30 letters at a time to him; and then he would dictate the 30 replies in a sequence; when the next batch of letters would be taken up. **For Dr Krishnaswamy, his eye blindness was a turning point in his career** and he came out on top of the situation.

Roy was one of the finest elevator servicemen that the company had. He had worked for the company for 26 years. He was so good that the company transferred his services to a country in the Middle East. One day when he and a colleague were attending to a problem, he saw his colleague lose his grip and fall down many floors to the basement. He lay there in a pool of blood—dead! Roy could not forget the sight—ever. From that day on, he just could not get up there—to attend to an elevator. He quit his job and went to Canada. He found it difficult to get a placement—because elevator repair was the only job he knew; and he did not want to do this. He now works as a postman in the little suburb of Montreal—and he is happy. He knows all the members of the community. They look forward to his call; many even invite him in for a cup of coffee. He has become a friend, philosopher and guide, especially to the elderly and lonely. He goes beyond the job of a postman. **A colleague's fall—a turning point in a career.**

Raghu did not mind that his son Anil did not opt to follow in his footsteps. Raghu owned a large and growing export business. Anil had decided to be a doctor. He was a bright student and he got admission to the Madras Medical College; completed his MBBS and then went to the US to specialise in surgery. We will never know what exactly happened. He says that he came to a point where he just could not stand the sight of blood. So he decided to give up medicine as a career; and got into journalism. He went back to college to pursue a new career. Today, he works as a medical copywriter for a large pharmaceutical company in New Jersey. **Somewhere, he came to a turning point in his career.**

At the age of 12, Kunal was given a camera by his uncle. This became his most valued possession. Kunal seldom went anywhere without his camera. And his father did not grudge him the film developing expense. In course of time, Kunal's photography improved; and he also set-up his own developing facilities. When he finished school, Kunal decided to opt for photography as a career. He went to the US and specialised in photography. He came back to India and set-up a studio for making audiovisual commercial presentations. He diversified into colour processing and then into high quality printing. His enterprise Son et Lumiere was a huge success. **All because of a turning point—the gift of a camera from his uncle.**

Carl was a good general surgeon and was building up a good practice in Bombay in the 50s. It was busy and successful life, when a personal tragedy occurred. His newborn daughter had a hairlip. At first, Carl and his wife did not know how to take it. But when the initial reaction died down, Carl decided he would go back to the UK and study what was then the new specialisation of plastic surgery. He came back after two years to operate on his own daughter and became one of the pioneers in this branch of surgery in the country. **The birth of his daughter was a turning point, in what would have been an otherwise successful but uneventful career.**

And, the birth of Malini, a spastic child, spurred Mithu Alur to start the Spastics Society of India, which has become one of India's most professionally run and largest institutions, with schools spread across the country, a research centre and a training workshop. Another turning point. **But, for this, Mithu might have been a housewife rather than a flag bearer.**

Accidents and strange incidents can launch careers, change them and even end them. It happens to every one of us. The important thing is to remain on top of the situation and come out a winner.

16

LITTLE THINGS SHOW UP
AND REVEAL THE REAL PERSON

*Some of the world's most successful master spies like Mata Hari, gave
themselves away on minutiae of an unguarded mannerism or response.*

—*ANONYMOUS*

It was a very wet day when I went for my first job interview. I
went to Worli, all the way from the Mumbai suburb of Chembur,
and arrived dripping from head to toe. When I was ushered in to
meet the personnel director, my hands trembled, both with the
cold and with nervousness. But the director immediately assessed
my discomfiture. He took my wet raincoat and hung it up, asked
whether I would prefer tea or coffee, poured a cup for me, talked
about the squally weather and Mumbai's flooded roads. And we
got smoothly into a conversation for the next hour and a half. It
was the little courtesies that showed him to be what he was—a
perfect gentleman. It is the little things that show up.

I had made an appointment for dinner at the Delhi Gymkhana
with my friend Brij, a retired Lt General. I had written to him
from Mumbai a week ahead of my visit. However, on the appointed day, I got caught up in a meeting which finished at eight in the
evening. Exhausted, I went back to my hotel and completely for-
got about the dinner appointment. When I returned to Mumbai,

I realised that I had not kept the appointment and made a note to write to Brij to apologise. But before I got around to doing that, I received a note from Brij. He wrote to say that he waited for a full hour and then left. He wondered what had happened to me and hoped that all was well!

Brij had shown his immense patience, and his ability not to jump to a conclusion. Also, to keep communication open and to wait for an explanation. Most people I know would not have done this. They would have been annoyed and upset, and would have decided not to have much to do with that person again. It is the little things that show up.

Mani had completed a round of three interviews for a senior assignment of commercial director with one of our client companies. He was a Ph.D. in management from the US and had worked there for 22 years before returning to India. I had thought it strange that he should decide to seek employment in India, leaving his wife and child in the US. But he said that his wife had a job there which she did not want to quit. Somehow, I had the sneaky feeling that something was wrong which he would not disclose. After he finished the interview, he came to my hotel room at 1 p.m. since he was to have lunch with me. He eyed the bottle of gin kept on the table. I saw this and asked if he wanted a drink. He said yes. After he had finished, I got up and suggested we go for lunch. He agreed. But could he have another quick one? I said yes and gave him the bottle. He poured half a glass, gulping it down neat. I knew then that he had a problem, and perhaps the reason why he had returned from the US. It is the little things that show up.

A prospective client had invited me to lunch at the Horse Shoe Restaurant in Mumbai. His office was close to the restaurant and he presumably often frequented it. When we took a table, I could sense the reluctance of the waiters around to attend to us. Finally, one of them came along. I heard him muttering to the others that the miser was going to be high on complaints and low on tips. After we had finished the meal and the bill was paid, the bearer brought back small coins in change. He insisted that my host take it, in a manner that just fell short of saying 'Please keep it, sir,

I think you need it more than I do'. One year later, I found that the client was reluctant to pay our consultancy fees. He defaulted for four months, till we stopped the work. The restaurant incident should have warned me. It is the little things that show up!

We had finished lunch at an expensive restaurant in a five-star hotel and were waiting for the waiter to bring the bill. It was then that I noticed that my host picked up a spoon and put it in his pocket. He saw that I had seen him in the act, and explained that he collected spoons from hotels as a hobby—'After all, they charge such atrocious prices. They can well afford to lose a spoon now and then.' It is the little things that count!

My friend Sonny was going to be married in Copenhagen to a Danish girl he had met at Cambridge. Sonny was a nuclear physicist, very intelligent and very forgetful. It was only when he was checking in at the SAS flight counter for Copenhagen, that he realised he had not taken a decent pair of shoes for the wedding. He asked the lady at the counter if there was any shop at the airport. He explained the situation. There was nothing that could be done. When he arrived at Copenhagen, Sonny was surprised to receive a parcel containing a pair of black shoes (which were happily the correct size) and a bouquet for the bride. Sonny has always flown SAS since.

When I rushed out of the hotel in Hyderabad because I was late for my flight to Chennai, I had assumed that my bag was already in the boot of the car which was to take me to the airport. It was only when I was at the airport that I realised that the bag was forgotten at the bell desk at the hotel. My friend promised to send the bag by the morning flight to Chennai. I, therefore, arrived at the Connemara Hotel at Chennai at 9 p.m. at night with only my briefcase. The receptionist was surprised that I had no luggage. I explained the situation. She was sympathetic. After filling in the registration form, I went up to the allotted room. Soon after I entered, the room boy rang the bell. He was there with a shaving kit, toothbrush and paste, comb, clothes for the night, and instructions to collect the clothes I was wearing, to be washed and delivered in the morning. I had not asked for this service. The hotel had done this on their own. It was a small gesture, but it showed thoughtfulness and care. I have stayed at the Connemara ever since, whenever I am in this town.

A student of Zen has to learn at the feet of his master for 10 years before he can graduate to be a teacher himself. There is the story of a student who had graduated, and went back after a few months to visit his teacher. Before entering the teacher's house on this rainy day, he left his wooden clogs and umbrella outside the door. The teacher asked him whether he had brought an umbrella. He said he had and that he had left the clogs and umbrella outside. The teacher asked him whether the umbrella was kept to the left or the right of the clogs. The student could not remember. Immediately, the student decided that he had not fully developed his sense of awareness, and that he would have to start another 10 years of apprenticeship!

Most of us, as managers, need to develop refinement in the little things. There is nothing that is not important or too minor to overlook. You will judge people and companies on these little things and others will judge you. It is the little windows that you peer through that give you a good view of the house.

17

BENEFICIAL ASSOCIATIONS
USING THE POWER OF SYNERGY

The epoch of individuality is concluded, and it is the duty of reformers to initiate the epoch of association. Collective man is omnipotent upon the earth he treads.

—GUISEPPE MAZZINI

An author I have greatly admired and learnt a lot from is Charles Vance, who wrote *Manager Today, Executive Tomorrow*. One of the 10 principles he propounds in this book is that 'from birth to death you are alone'.[1] You may have parents to help you up to a point; you may have your wife or children to help you at other stages in your life; or you may have bosses, colleagues, subordinates, friends and acquaintances to give you a helping hand at various times; but essentially, each one of us has to handle our own affairs. We must depend on ourselves. Samuel Smiles' dictum that 'God helps those who help themselves' still holds true for all of us.

---

[1] Vance, Charles C. 1974. *Manager Today, Executive Tomorrow*. New York, USA: McGraw-Hill Book Company.

And yet, it is also true that there is very little that any one of us can do alone. Most of us, and certainly corporate executives, need to get work done through other people. We need to develop two qualities very acutely—to recognise a good idea or person, and to make the best use of talent, when we find it.

Al Ries and Jack Trout have developed this theme very effectively in their book *Horse Sense*. Ries and Trout have written many books in the past, all very popular, on marketing strategy. But in *Horse Sense*, they have gone further, into the realms of marketing yourself—the individual.

Ries and Trout are emphatic that the **key to your success is always somebody else**. Even when you have a great idea or a great product, you are counting on others to recognise the value of the idea or the product.

A salesman never makes a sale. Someone else has to purchase the product. What's true in selling products is also true in selling yourself. Somebody else has to first recognise your good qualities and then 'buy' you by giving you a job, a promotion or even entering into a business partnership.

Ries and Trout believe that in the course of a typical career, this selling and buying process takes place many times. Their surveys show that the average person needs to sell himself seven times between the first big job and retirement. It can be a difficult and frustrating process—because sometimes the timing can be brutal. Let's say that you are just fired. At that moment in your career when you need the most self-confidence, you have the least. How do you sell yourself if you're not sold on yourself?

It is suggested that one easy way out is to sell yourself once to someone who can do something for you. They give many examples from corporate life in the US. They also refer to Dan Quayle and how he rode to glory on the back of George Bush. We have our own examples of beneficial associations—R.K. Dhawan with Indira Gandhi, George with Rajiv Gandhi, Jayalalitha and MGR. Similarly, you will also find numerous examples in industry. This is because you cannot ride alone. Finding a person to ride with—whether mentor, partner or spouse—is an easy way to the winners' circle. But at the same time, it is also a tricky ride on the track, because the person you are riding with could find you expendable if you become a liability in any way.

Using a partner can also help to build a powerful combination in any business. Two people usually do better than either one alone. Yet, if you look around, you often see loners.

A loner starts out well, with the advantage of youth, enthusiasm, energy and a fresh approach. As he/she gets older, the ego grows with the income. As the ego begins to overwhelm ability, the loner becomes a pompous know-it-all and objectivity is smothered. This is where partners can help to keep you down to earth. A partner can supply the objectivity that will keep the ego in check. You can accomplish things together that you wouldn't be able to alone.

This synergistic effect has been proved over and over again in the history of business partnerships—Jobs and Wozmak of Apple, Gates and Allen of Microsoft, Hewlett & Packard who started in a garage and became a $12 billion company with 95,000 employees and offices around the world.

Lee Iacocca did very little himself. His great ability was to recognise the talent of others. He identified the Mustang, the Ford model which would become a bestseller. Iacocca did not design the Mustang. He did not engineer the Mustang. He recognised the merits of the design executed by Joe Oros, Gail Halderman and David Ash.

The result: *Forbes* in September 1964 reported Ford's Mustang as the hottest car in the auto business today and Lee Iacocca as the hottest business executive.

A sales manager today, however brilliant he/she may be, cannot do the job of five, 10 or a 100 salesmen that he/she may oversee. Even if he/she improves the performance of 10 salesmen by 10 per cent, it will be far more profitable than improving only his/her own selling ability by 30 per cent. The sales manager or any other manager must get work done through others.

And yet, the executive must rely on his own mindset, knowledge and skills for basic sustenance. If people desert him, he should be capable of riding the storm alone, for a while. Indira Gandhi did this when she was in political wilderness. So did Charles de Gaulle. They knew they had to lead people and get the work done by them. And when they were left alone, they accepted it with that final refrain of confidence—'I will return.' The real key to success is not just believing in yourself but, in greater measure, also believing in someone else, or others!

18

Enhancing Career Option with Networking
Extending the Reach

Those who are most content, generally do not have the best of everything. They try to make the best of everything.

—Anonymous

I once read an article in World Executive Digest where the authors said that Networking is often mistaken for politicking, kissing up, sharing ideas and exchanging secrets. Whatever you call it, and whatever your opinion of the age-old art of collaborating, it is still important for career growth, especially with associates in your own organisation. They add that many people equate the management network with corporate politics. Maybe they're partially correct, but networking is not just a matter of getting plugged into your company's rumour mill. That's a waste of time and energy. Networking is **the creation of a managerial network you can use to enhance your career options.**

Most executives do not know how to build networks or how to use them judiciously. These executives belong to those categories of introverted-thinking. Intro-intuitive, Intro-feeling or Intro-sensing, listed in the Myers-Briggs Type Indicators.

But there is a smaller percentage of executives who do know how to build networks and make use of them, and they use these well to climb up the corporate ladder.

The most obvious one we see is the old school tie network. In many companies, there are attachments among the Doon School clan (we saw a lot of it in Rajiv Gandhi's 'kitchen cabinet') or among the St Stephen's, St Xavier's or the Mayo college clan. They get introduced to one another, or even get recommendations from one another due to their old school ties; although they may not get promotions within corporations on this basis.

Managers develop networks by joining professional organisations. It could be the Institute of Engineers, the Institute of Industrial Engineers, or the Institute of Chartered Accountants or the local management association. In fact, many management consultants try to develop a network of prospects through an active role in the local management association, through which they get exposure to and work with managers in the corporate sector, who are their potential customers. Other managers take great interest in a professional organisation just prior to retirement, because they intend to set-up shop as consultants and would therefore like to build a large network with practising managers well in advance. Still others build a network so that it will help them to get personal exposure for another, better career opportunity that may arise elsewhere in the industry.

These are networks that are developed within the same profession, 'profession' being understood either in a narrow sense (chartered accountants) or in a broader sense (management associations).

There are other networks that are developed at a common interest but socially compatible level. The common interest is community service, as with the Rotary and Lions Clubs, but it also requires a certain social compatibility and acceptability to be admitted. These networks help to expose you to other professions and widen the spectrum.

Roy, who always sports a Rotary lapel pin on his coat, struck up a conversation with a stranger in the underground metro in London. This stranger was also a Rotarian from Australia, visiting London on business. They became acquainted as they shared a common interest. Today, they do business with each other. The international ramifications of the Rotary network had helped Roy!

In the industry network, such as the Organisation of Pharmaceutical Producers of India, representatives of a particular industry meet, get to know each other and discuss common strategies and representations. It is the same with the Cement Manufacturers Association and the Tyres Manufacturers Association. These organisations help you to develop a network to obtain quick information, to share ideas and even to get exposure to another assignment within the industry.

There are narrow-band status-position networks such as the informal groups of chief executives of medium to large firms in Mumbai, who meet once a month to discuss common problems and exchange ideas. They also have picnics twice a year with their families to enable the closer establishment of bonds between themselves. This helps them to be available to each other for advice, for guidance, as sounding boards as well as for help.

The International Association of Young Presidents admits as members those who have become presidents of corporations (of a certain minimum size in turnover) before the age of 40 years. All these young and successful members can thus be provided with an opportunity to network with one another and to help each other.

Networks are sought to be built even by communities, especially in a large city such as Mumbai. The Mathurs have an annual picnic in Mumbai every year and a large number of families join in. It gives an opportunity for the young men to meet the young women of the community and for their parents to meet each other. Networks are built and marriages are 'made on earth' rather than in heaven!

C.D. Tam, of Motorola in Southeast Asia and the first Asian to get a top regional management position in Motorola, says that 'to constantly broaden his global perspective, he communicates regularly with other Motorola people around the world, mostly by electronic mail'. Tam believes in networking within the company and admits that this has been one of the main reasons for his great success.

Lee Tom Perry in *Offensive Strategy—Competing Head to Head* explains that opportunists first form, then use, networks of relationships to help identify and evaluate new opportunities. It was on this premise that Trammel Crow succeeded in building a large real estate business with the philosophy that 'I'd rather be one strong man among other strong men than a strong man alone'. Crow's network sustained an incredible record of success for his company and for himself.

The internet has opened up tremendous opportunities, unimagined only 15 years ago, for networking. People now use Facebook and Twitter; they use their own blog; they use networks like LinkedIn and some of the others. It gives them a worldwide reach, which goes way beyond the physical form we had earlier known.

However, networking, to be really effective, ideally requires the existence of a certain equality of status within a broad band. Generally, you cannot network with people who are much below or above you—that would evolve into a system of mentoring.

Networking also ideally requires a certain reciprocity—to be able to ask something of someone, you should be able to do something for them. It is expected to be a two-way street.

Suresh had joined a small management consultancy company as a senior consultant, on the basis that he would be able to bring in clients and have a share of the fee revenue. It was the profit-sharing arrangement which appealed to Suresh because he had not gone too far in his corporate career despite his excellent academic qualifications. Since Suresh played tennis with the chairman of an industrial group most mornings, and bridge every weekend with some very powerful industrialists, he thought that getting business would not be very difficult. At the end of one year, Suresh quit the consultancy company to rejoin industry. He had not attracted any business at all. His acquaintances in high positions were happy to play with him, because he was a good tennis and bridge player, but they did not look at him as an equal or an associate in business. The network on which he had relied so much just did not exist!

Networking is very important for success as a manager. However, networking, especially outside one's own company, needs some parity of status, ability to reciprocate and mutual respect and trust.

19

GRABBING OPPORTUNITIES
NEEDS GRASP AND REACH

The strongest of all warriors are these two—Time and Patience.
—LEO TOLSTOY, WAR AND PEACE

Reading Ries and Trout's *Horse Sense* made me think of all the boys in school who had consistently stood first in class, year after year. I have not heard of most of them for a long, long time. Some joined the IFS and have yet to become ambassadors. Some joined the private sector and have yet to become CEOs. By the age of 55 years, they should have. Some became doctors and lawyers and I know that they could do with some more 'practice' or 'clientele' just to make ends meet.

What put me into this reverie was Ries's statement that 'in the dairy, cream rises to the top. In daily life, it's generally not true'. It's mostly milk at the top of the corporate bottle. Intelligence is a two-edged sword. Too little and you can't cope with the corporate paperwork: writing memos, travel arrangements. Too much and you are out of touch with reality. You suffer from the absent-minded professor syndrome.

Top executives come from the middle of the IQ curve. As the college president said to the faculty, 'Be nice to your *A* students because they will come back and be your colleagues, but be exceptionally nice to your B and C students because they will come back and give us a new auditorium and a new science building.'

Peter McColough, former chairman of Xerox, made the same point about his Harvard School class of 1949. 'The record of accomplishment corresponds negatively with the standing in the class.' The top people did not do that well. The one-third in the middle did. The guys who got the highest marks tended to be in the middle in accomplishment.

Why is this? Why does success in the classroom generally not correlate with success in a profession? The smarter the people are, the more they depend on themselves. After all, they know everything. They depend only on themselves to get ahead. Less intelligent people are more likely to look for others to help them up the ladder, and to look for opportunities and grab them.

Swamy was working at the Mumbai Airport as a traffic assistant. One day a friend approached him to say that his international company chairman was arriving and could he somehow manage to get the local managing director to receive and welcome him inside the 'No visitors allowed' area? Pulling the right strings, Swamy managed to do this. The managing director, Whitby, was very appreciative. When the group was leaving the airport, he told Swamy to feel welcome and see him any time at the office, if he needed anything. A week later, Swamy did call Whitby and fixed an appointment. He told Whitby that he was fed up of the traffic assistant job and that it was also a dead end. Was there anything he could do, with his pass class B.A. degree, in this large toiletries conglomerate? Swamy was hired as regional sales manager for west India. Whitby felt that with his people skills, Swamy would perform—and Swamy did. He rose to be general manager of a division before he left the company to become general manager of another company. Had he ignored the invitation to see Whitby and considered the invitation merely as a social nicety, Swamy would have perhaps been a senior traffic assistant 15 years later.

I never wrote articles earlier. All I wrote as a working executive were memos, minutes and reports. Then a student at a management college where I taught marketing married a journalist.

She spoke to her husband about me, because he was desperately looking around for someone to write a regular column on Marketing for *BusinessWorld*. He asked me. I said I would try. That was 20 years ago. I have been writing a column every month ever since—and some more. I had grabbed an opportunity, and not just said 'No. I've never done it before'.

'Life is a cobweb', said Ross Perot, the billionaire who was a US presidential candidate. 'The lines cross at funny angles. Whether you are successful or not doesn't depend on how good your plans are, especially those five-year strategic plans business schools teach. **Success depends on how you react to unexpected opportunities.**'

Tom Peters also echoes the same idea, 'I don't like the whole notion of career planning. I've never had a formula, never had a life plan. I've taken advantage of luck (opportunity?) when it came along.' And he adds, 'Luck (opportunities?) is 98 per cent of the deal.' Tom Peters, at a lecture fee of US $60,000 a day, with a 100 engagements a year, should know!

And opportunities do not just arise in the environment. They are not presented to us by others, as the earlier incidents show. They can be inherent in us. They can be accidents that we may take to be calamities but that can be turned into opportunities. A young singer with a fine soprano voice was assigned to perform *The End of a Perfect Day* for admiring relatives. When his adolescent voice cracked and broke at the family gathering, he discovered he had the ability to make people laugh. The singer-cum-comedian was Bob Hope!

The goal-oriented person would have said, 'I'm not going to let this incident stop me from becoming a professional singer.' The hard work-oriented person would have said, 'I have to practise more.' But successful people take advantage of accidents. They see an opportunity in a calamity and grab it.

20

THE IMPORTANCE OF BEING A TEAM PLAYER
LEVERAGING THE POWER OF MANY

*The greatest fear for a leader, is to look back over his shoulder,
and find no one following him.*
—FRANKLIN ROOSEVELT

In our country everyone wants to be a leader. To be a leader, is to be a neta. And once you are a neta then all the other prerequisites follow. Position, status, money, however, it may be earned, security guards, large accommodation and servants. However, everyone cannot become a leader. When one does become a leader, it may not be on a permanent basis. Leadership is always transient. Most of us spend most of the time as followers. To be a good follower, you have to be a good team player. To be a good leader, also, you have to be a good follower first.

The ability to train and collect good followers, i.e. good team players, makes for the difference between success and failure. Japan emerged as a great nation because the Japanese developed into good team players. So did the South Koreans. So did the Singaporeans and the Germans. Indians are great individuals and perhaps superior to the Japanese on a one-to-one basis. But Indians fail miserably against the Japanese and Singaporeans on a team-to-team basis. Does this show in our sports performance? Perhaps, in some ways, it does. While we may win medals and championships in individual events like rifle shooting or wrestling—India's performance in team events like hockey, football and cricket is miserable. Just imagine—we cannot put together an outstanding team of 12 persons out of a population of one billion people. Yet, it is teams of people that make the difference. Alfred Sloan, the man who built General Motors into the biggest and most successful automobile company in the world, once boasted 'Take my assets, but leave me my organization, and in five years, I'll have it all back.'

Sloan made that statement because he knew that more than money in the bank; and more than sophisticated technology; or the lowest price on its products; it is the people who work at a company, who make the difference between success and failure.

For any organisation to succeed, government or corporate, the people in it must work together. If they do, they can work wonders. In any field, a team that pulls together will beat a talented collection of individuals.

It is not easy to create that kind of teamwork. People don't always get on well—and there is friction and conflict that can hinder the team process. It takes a lot of effort to work harmoniously with other people. But it can be done if you follow John McDonnell's simple four-point formula.

(1) Use empathy. See other points of view. The moment a worker complains about an excessive workload, we jump to the conclusion that he is a 'whiner' or a 'trade unionist'. Maybe the workload is very high. Would you be able to handle this load yourself? Is there something you can do to help? If you take an interest in your co-workers as human beings—including their life outside work, their interests, hopes, dreams, aspirations, fears and hobbies—you will find it easier to get along with them.

(2) **Recognize that nobody's perfect.** We are all human beings and we are all imperfect. When someone makes a
mistake, don't criticise or belittle him Focus on correct-
ing the mistake. Try to be helpful. Abraham Lincoln once
said, 'He has the right to criticise who has the heart to
help.' Nobody's perfect. Next week you may be the one
who makes a blunder.

(3) **Don't be afraid to say, 'I'm sorry'.** If you make a mistake,
admit it. Don't try to put the blame on someone else. If
you always make yourself look good at the expense of others,
you destroy morale and team spirit. Others will be more
willing to help you if they know you are honest about
admitting your mistakes. In fact, the ability to admit a
mistake is the mark of a great man. It is cowards who try to
pass the buck—and always show it is someone else's fault.
Over a period of time, this gets exposed. People begin to
recognise the real you. You cannot fool all the people all
the time.

(4) **Be willing to compromise.** Just like in a good marriage,
the member of a successful team has to know how to compromise. When someone is sick, you may have to work
extra time. Every individual voluntarily gives up some of
his needs, for the good for the team.

Have you ever seen the great football player, Ronaldo, of
Brazil, play? He is always a marked man on the playing field.
There are two or three opposition players always surrounding him.
They know that if he gets the ball under control, it means a sure
goal. So Ronaldo works his way up the field, dodging through the
defense, until he sees an unmarked and free team player to whom
he passes the ball. This team player has all the time and freedom
to shoot the goal. Ronaldo does not bother that he himself did
not shoot the goal. What is important to him is that the Brazil
team wins.

Establishing a true spirit of cooperation means understanding
human nature. We all have good days and bad days. We all have
our strengths and weaknesses. When you accept people for what

they are and try to focus on what's good for the organisation, the little frictions won't bother you as much.

Teambuilding is contagious. Once a few members of the team start working well together, the others follow the example. Success breeds more success. Before you know it, you are part of something unique and great—a united group of people, working towards a common goal. McDonnell says, that's when you have a winning team.

The information technology (IT) industry has begun to boom in India. Since team working is critical to IT success, Indians will be forced to become good team members and good followers, before they become good leaders!

21

Becoming an Effective Manager And Not Just an Efficient Manager

The world will belong to passionate, driven Leaders—people who not only have enormous amounts of energy, but who can energise those whom they lead.
—*Jack Welch, CEO, General Electric*

Peter Drucker, the high priest of modern management, has repeatedly emphasised one point: that an executive must be effective and not just efficient. The dictum may seem trite and obvious but if you look around your own organisation, the chances are that this obvious requirement is often overlooked. Most times, executives become ineffective for a variety of reasons.

One reason is that they do not know or have forgotten how to set priorities. Executives cannot distinguish between what they must do and what they want to do. And more often than not, they succumb to the temptation of doing the latter. In the process, more pressing and urgent problems are delayed. Excuses are then used to justify the delay and we have a situation of the cat chasing its tail.

Many executives do not know how to manage time. They work harder, but not smarter. This comes from a wrong sense of priorities. They are not able to schedule time properly, or allot the right amount of time for the right purpose and to allow for contingencies. They are constantly chasing the clock and before they know it, it's seven in the evening and time to go home.

Another important reason why many executives are efficient but not effective, is that they do not devote enough time to mastering the basic skills needed for managerial effectiveness, e.g. skills of dictation, rapid reading and delegation.

In one of the companies where I worked, the managing director impressed many by the fact that he was the first to arrive at the office and the last to leave. He seemed to devote almost all his waking hours to the company, and worked hard. Later, I discovered that he could not dictate letters. He wrote every letter by hand before it was typed. If it was a letter to a government department, he spent half a day over it. If it was a letter to be sent abroad to corporate international headquarters, he spent more than half a day over it. Meanwhile, his secretary sat in her room doing her knitting, crochet or whatever, waiting for her boss's handiwork. How did a poor writer like him then get into the managing director's seat? Probably more by accident than by design!

Surveys conducted by our consulting firm have shown that the average reading speed of executives in India is about 250 words per minute, when, in fact, it should be around 500. President Kennedy is believed to have had a phenomenal speed of 1,500 words per minute. He was not born with this capacity; he cultivated it. For Indian executives, the lesson is that poor reading speed erodes 50 per cent of one's time. If two or three hours can be saved every day, it works out to over 40 days a year of additional time!

Delegation is another weak spot in the executive character in India. This probably has something to do with the shortage of 'good jobs'. Many people, therefore, try to protect their own jobs and keep their subordinates in a subordinate position to prevent them from emerging as serious competitors. This objective is achieved by two methods. The more primeval of them is to repeatedly and overtly reinforce that you are the boss. The other is to deny information to subordinates who are perceived as rivals. The boss thus withholds some information so that he/she gains information power and commands respect, or so he/she thinks!

This prima donna attitude of many executives often results in inadequate preparation of successors. It also results in the boss taking on more work than he/she can handle. Loss of effectiveness is the result. Look around, and one will find sales managers who double as salesmen, production managers pitching in as foremen and finance controllers playing internal auditors.

There is yet another fallout of this conflict between efficiency and effectiveness. It is the so-called efficient people—who have worked hard, sacrificed family life for work life and generally refused to delegate jobs—who find themselves left behind 20 years later. They stagnate while their effective colleagues move up without seeming to work so hard.

In the end, the efficient executives are the ones to feel frustrated. Feeling unappreciated, they spread the cancer of dissatisfaction to new entrants and younger executives. Effectiveness is the ability to get the job done, and to ensure and improve productivity. It means doing the right thing, whereas efficiency means doing things right. It is ideal to have both, but if that is not possible, then effectiveness is better.

It is difficult to enumerate all the factors that go into building effectiveness. But if an executive were to set proper priorities, manage time, improve reading speed and develop a sense of confidence and security about his job (and therefore delegate and develop subordinates to be as good as and even better than himself/herself), he/she would be well on his/her way to becoming an effective manager.

22

Opportunities to Learn
They Are Many and Varied

Still I am learning.
—*Michelangelo, 1475–1564*

Some time ago, I was watching an old management film called *The Professional*. Van Johnson, the well-known Hollywood actor of yesteryears who featured in many westerns, plays the lead role in this movie. In one of the scenes, Johnson is told that to be a real professional, he should have 'the will to learn and keep on learning throughout his professional career'. Johnson wryly responds that it seems that he would now have to attend night school, or worse, obtain a Ph.D. to be a professional. His senior colleague clarifies that this is not what is meant. He says that Johnson has been 'learning' all these years (albeit not in the 'formal sense') through attending seminars, trade shows, industry conventions, sales conference, etc. Johnson thus had several opportunities for 'learning' and yet, was not aware of it. He has, therefore, probably missed out on getting the full benefit of the 'learning exposure'.

I have been doing some development work in change processes for a large company. I have consistently found that the higher the level of management, the less they are willing to learn. Workshops for vice-presidents and general managers are poorly attended, those for middle managers better attended and the workshops for junior managers have the best attendance.

The junior-most managers are mostly recent graduates out of college. Their knowledge levels are high although their experience may be limited. The senior managers have graduated 30-years-ago and the world has gone through a sea change in that time. If anyone needs reorientation, through informal and formal learning, it is the senior managers. And yet, paradoxically, they are the most reluctant to learn.

What is the system of informal learning? It requires an open mind and the ability to learn from superiors, peers and subordinates. It requires a certain sublimation of the ego and a humility that 'the more one knows, the more one knows what one does not know'. And the opportunities for 'learning from the streets' are enormous—if only one keeps the 'windows of the mind' open.

When I was posted to Jabalpur 40 years ago, I went out on my first day of fieldwork for Glaxo. At that time there was a big market war for narrow spectrum antibiotics between Glaxo, Pfizer and Sarabhai. At the first retail outlet I visited, I met Rodrigues, a senior representative from Pfizer. He had a paternal look and, as I discovered later, was the most respected medical representative in Jabalpur, in fact, in the whole Madhya Pradesh area. He asked me whether I was the new Glaxo representative for the area and whether I was new to the profession. The answer to both questions was 'yes'. He offered to take me around and introduce me to the leading doctors in Jabalpur. He did that over three days. In some cases, he even requested the doctors to give me 'prescription support' since I was new to the profession. At the end of the third day he said, 'Walter, you should now be able to manage on your own. It was nice working with you. From now on, we will have a good fight in the market-place.'

Rodrigues was so up-to-date with his medical knowledge that every year he addressed doctors on the 'latest developments in medicine', although he himself was not a doctor. He taught me early in life the true meaning of professionalism. He was knowledgeable, kept learning and helped others in the profession to keep getting better. He knew that 'he never stoops low, who stoops to help a child'.

I had just come in from a walk through the extensive gardens of the West End Hotel in Bangalore. It was 8:30 a.m. in the morning and as I passed through the lounge, I saw Sharu sitting on one of the sofas with a briefcase on his lap and writing furiously. I went up to him and asked him if his room was not ready and if he would like to use my room for the time being. 'Oh no', he said. He had come only for the day and was leaving that evening. His marketing director was, in fact, staying in the hotel but he did not want to disturb him until he had got ready for the day. He would ring him up at 9 a.m. and then have a wash and move to the conference hall. Sharu was the managing director of the company. He could have booked a room, but he did not want to waste money. He could have spoken to his junior colleague earlier, but he showed consideration and courtesy. In just five minutes he taught me some valuable lessons, by his own example, provided I was willing to learn.

A few years ago I was travelling from Singapore to Bombay. One of India's leading industrialists requested me to help his daughter who was travelling on the same flight. I had gone to Singapore on work for this same industrialist. He was staying back while I was returning early. When I got on to the plane, I looked around and found she was not there in the business class. When the plane took off, I went to the first class and she was not there either. I finally decided to take a walk down the 'club class' and saw her there. Surprise must have been written all over my face when I said, 'What Asha, you are here? I thought you had missed the flight.' She replied very simply, 'You know, uncle, Dad allows us to travel only economy. He says we have not yet earned a higher class travel.' A simple incident taught me a lesson. My eminent client was sending a signal to his children and to his company. 'You have to earn your privileges. They cannot be taken for granted.' The rich man's son syndrome is the worst disability that can befall any person. It kills the ability to strive to attain. I had learnt another lesson.

It was my first visit to the Jet Company in Central India. I was studying their systems and procedures to acquaint myself with their methods of working. When I was questioning them about their appraisal system, I was surprised to find that in this small

₹350 million family-owned company, they had adopted a system where the juniors also appraised their superiors. The pace was set by the managing director who was also the owner of the company. Every four months, i.e. thrice a year, he had a half-hour session with each department head who reported to him where they gave him honest feedback about his operational style—both strengths and weaknesses. It was done briefly and courteously. The managing director took no offence. In fact, he tried to take action on areas for improvement, which he would not have been as aware of otherwise, without this exercise. It takes courage to face an evaluation, especially from those who report to you, and especially when you own the company. This managing director taught me a valuable lesson in self-analysis and correction.

There is a flower vendor at the traffic lights at the corner of Church gate and Marine Drive in Mumbai. The lights change every three minutes. He has just those three minutes in which to identify prospects in passing cars, demonstrate his product, create a desire to buy, negotiate the price, close the sale and collect the money. He has taught me more lessons on the 'theory of selling' than all the tomes that have been written on the subject.

There are opportunities for learning all the time—at conferences and seminars, in books and magazines, on TV and in the open university of life. If we blind ourselves and close the doors to 'fresh winds from the outside', as Mahatma Gandhi once suggested, we will have shown an unwillingness to learn or to change, and therefore not be eligible for the appellation of 'professional'.

23

THE NEED TO LEARN/UNLEARN/ RELEARN
A LIFELONG PURSUIT

It is now an exciting world full of opportunities. But you have to be nimble and move quickly to grab those opportunities. You also have to know what you can do and what you cannot do. You have to further know what you could do; if you retrained yourself to do the new things you need to/want to do.

The key to success in the 21st century is Learn/Unlearn/Relearn (LUR). This is the essence of *The Fifth Disciple* that popular book for managers, by Peter Senge. Did he say very much that is New? Really, no. He just highlighted what we might already know; but may have forgotten.

In the formula LUR—lies the key to changing careers, creating excitement and moving on in life to do what you really want to do—with passion and determination!

Nikhil did his MBA at a business school in USA; then worked at Citibank for three years in New York. He then got tired of the world of finance and banking. So what did he do? He liked the food business. He wanted to start a speciality restaurant in Mumbai, India—his hometown. He assessed there would be a window open for Thai/Vietnamese food. So he went to Thailand and Vietnam and spent many months learning the art of cooking these two cuisines.

He came back to Mumbai and began a catering service for parties. It was a premium service with food, crockery/cutlery and bearers. This went on for some years—and was a great success.

He then graduated into starting his own restaurant—Busaba— at a premium location in Colaba, Mumbai.

Nikhil had changed his direction. He had moved from banking to the food business. He had learnt/unlearnt/relearned. It was not easy to change channels. But he had discipline and he had passion!

I met Mohan on a flight from Mumbai to Chicago. By chance, he was sitting next to me and, as happens on these long flights, we began a conversation. This conversation kept me in rapt attention for a few hours when he told me his life story. Mohan now was in saffron clothes of a Sadhu. He lived in Chicago. He has been in the USA for 24 years. But he was not always a Sadhu.

Mohan had done electrical engineering from IIT Kharagpur. He had then emigrated to the USA, like most of his classmates. He joined a large Fortune 500 company and had a successful career as an electrical engineer. And then, he got a new idea. For the thread ceremony of the son of a friend, they just could not get a Hindu priest. Those that were listed were too busy. They were booked eight months in advance! Mohan, now single, 31-years-old, looked at this as an opportunity—to serve the community and yet, also have adequate financial rewards!

Mohan is now a Hindu priest in Chicago. He resigned his job, came to India and trained himself in all the rituals over a period of two years. Then he donned his saffron robes and went back to Chicago. Mohan had been a priest for six years when I met him on the flight. He allowed me to take a glance at his diary—he was booked for functions for 10 months in advance. His clients were from as far as Florida in the South, New Jersey in the East and Silicon Valley, California in the West. His travel was all paid for and charged a fat fee! He now earned much more than he did at a Fortune 500 company.

Mohan had changed direction. In a very unusual way. Once again showing that you can LUR to tread new paths.

A career is not necessarily forever. Change is available for those who have discipline and who have passion! And to those that dare!

24

MANAGEMENT OF TIME
A KEY ELEMENT FOR SUCCESS

*Rich or poor, beautiful or ugly—we have all been allotted the same
quantum of time per day to use or to waste.*

—ANONYMOUS

Many managers fail to become effective executives for just one reason. They are poor managers of time. As Joe Batten keeps repeating in the film *Manage Your Time*, executives keep working harder, but they could have and should work smarter. Most executives know they face a problem on this front, so they read books, see films and attend training programmes on time management. But while some among them change their old ways, others seem to find it difficult to get rid of old habits and imbibe new ones.

Some executives do not even realise they have a problem and go on achieving results disproportionate to the effort they had put in, and wonder why they never achieved what they wanted.

A colleague of mine called Arjun, who was a purchase executive, as well as president of the Amateur Film Society in the city, got so involved in the running of the society that he had little time to concentrate on the job he was paid to do. He came to work late and left early; had no time to meet suppliers or identify new or alternative sources and was rightly bypassed twice for a promotion to the next grade. He could not manage his time because he had the wrong priorities—his priority was his hobby rather than his profession.

Another colleague, Arun, was marketing manager of a large consumer product company. He spent all his time writing or changing the 'copy' for advertisements designed by the agency. He spent hours in meetings with the agency team, chopping and changing, much to the annoyance and frustration of his own marketing director and the ad agency personnel. Arun had no time to really think of a marketing strategy, distribution problems, sales force recruitment, training, coaching and motivation. Again, he had the wrong priorities—he spent time on what he liked to do, rather than on what he needed to do. His advertising agency past, was clinging to him, or the other way round.

Robin, a senior manager with a large multinational company, felt that the more committees he was included on, the more important he became. So he actively sought inclusion on every conceivable committee. The result was that he spent so much time in meetings—many of them useless from his point of view—that his branch managers and department staff found it difficult to find time to communicate with him. Robin spent his time seeking intra-corporate exposure and, consequently, could not find time for the 'meat of his job'.

Most executives try to adopt all the standard techniques to manage time—setting priorities, distinguishing between the urgent and the important, bunching jobs, blocking off calls and allocating time to think and plan. But all this comes to nought if the executive is unable to say 'no', and with a smile! That way one not only saves time, but also keeps a friend. Most of us are not able to do this. We are brusque when we say 'no', or we are pleasant and constrained to say 'yes'.

I had gone to meet Sam, the marketing director of a large chemicals company, because we were to have a meeting at 10 a.m. I reached a little early and was promptly taken to the conference room. The two other participants were present. But the marketing director was not. He came in at about 10.15, looking very apologetic. 'Can you please give me another 15 minutes?'

he asked, 'One of our biggest distributors from Bihar is in town and decided to drop in to say 'hello'. The bane of a courtesy visit! He had come in without an appointment. There was nothing important to discuss. Yet, Sam could not muster the courage to say he had an important meeting and couldn't spend time with him. He could not say 'no'.

Shyam is the marketing manager of a large cement company. He is in the office till 8.30 p.m. every evening and returns to his distant suburban home at about 10 p.m. His explanation is that cement dealers in the city are relatively free after 6.30 p.m., which is when they come to see him about any problems they may have. Shyam has not yet sorted out the truth for himself—whether they really come at that time because Shyam is available or because that is a convenient time for them. Shyam has not been able to say 'no'.

Some years ago in the US, I wanted to meet Theodore Levitt, a professor at Harvard University, to discuss some issues. I was introduced to him by a common friend. I phoned to ask him if we could meet. He asked me what it was about, and then asked whether we could discuss it on the telephone right then. He was very pleasant about it.

We talked for nearly half an hour and finished what needed to be done. I had saved a trip to the college from Boston and he had saved time as well.

All salesmen can collect outstandings by using strong arm tactics, and lose a customer in the process. This does not need any special skills. But a great salesman is one who can collect outstandings while retaining the customer—by collecting with a smile.

In the same vein, a good executive is one who can say 'no' pleasantly, thus retaining friendly and cordial relations and not allowing others to waste his time.

The executive's inability to manage time is reflected to the outsider through many indicators.

(1) You telephone him and are told, 'I'm sorry he's in a meeting!'
(2) His secretary says he will call you back and he doesn't.
(3) You write to him and he replies after a month.

(4) You write a congratulations/condolence letter; he doesn't acknowledge it at all (may also be a reflection on his breeding and background).
(5) You go to meet him with an appointment and he calls you in 45 minutes after the appointed time.
(6) His staff finds it difficult to spend time with him.
(7) His desk is piled with papers.
(8) There are always more than two people in his room talking to him about two different matters, a conversation which is constantly interrupted by incoming telephone calls.

Peter Drucker provides us with a useful concept of 'discretionary time'—the period in which the manager exercises a choice over what he is doing. It is for the executive to protect and even enlarge this discretionary time sector. And he can do this by preventing time wasters.

(1) over-supervising or under-supervising subordinates
(2) starting jobs without first planning
(3) scheduling less important work before more important work
(4) leaving jobs half done
(5) doing jobs which can be delegated to someone else or to a machine
(6) doing unproductive jobs or what is not a part of his real job
(7) spending a disproportionate amount of time on areas of special interest
(8) getting bogged down in too much paperwork
(9) pursuing unachievable or low-yield projects
(10) keeping an open door too open—failing to anticipate crisis
(11) chasing trivial data when important data is already in
(12) attending or conducting meetings which prolong unnecessarily
(13) socialising too much between tasks
(14) handling too wide a range of duties
(15) never analysing one's own use of time

But there are other ways to stretch discretionary time—by

(1) planning for the day
(2) learning to skim reports and developing the ability for fast reading
(3) being selective in reading journals
(4) using the telephone to save writing
(5) delegating all repetitive tasks
(6) learning how to use idle time, even if it is brief moments
(7) blocking out the quietest hours for creative work.

It is such executives who have mastered the art of time management who seem to get work done as well as enjoy themselves. They are the envy of the vast majority who just look on and say—'I wonder how he does it. Where does he find the time?'

25

Effective Communication
The Hub of Fayol's Wheel

Courage is what it takes to stand up and speak. Courage is also what it takes to sit down and listen.
—Winston Churchill (1874–1965)

Many people talk about the art of handling people. Very few of us actually know how to handle people well. It starts with the family, expands to the neighbourhood and extends to the corporation. Good human relations depend on two important requirements—the ability to use empathy and the ability to communicate.

Most of us find it easy to be apathetic to people around us. It is also convenient—'I don't care', 'What does it matter to me?', 'How am I concerned?', 'It's better not to get involved'. Some of us may be able to squeeze out some 'sympathy', to gush over with great sorrow, perhaps even shed a few tears, bleary eyes filled with sadness. But it is not easy to strike the balance in between—of being empathetic.

Empathy is the ability to put yourself in the other person's shoes and to see the problem from his point of view. It is also good, and sometimes necessary, to get the other person to see your point of view. The old Red Indian prayer encapsulated the essence so beautifully in a few lines:

Great Spirit, grant that I may not criticise my neighbour, Until I have walked a mile in his mocassins.

The ability to communicate is also critical to ensuring good human relations. We have made considerable progress in the *technology* of communication: starting with the printing press, going to the telegraph and telephone, radio and television, facsimile, Internet and now the use of satellite communication. But it would seem that we have made very little progress in the *essence* of communication.

The increased number of separations between husbands and wives, estrangements between parents and children, the never-ending quarrels between nations and between religions within the same nation, and sects within the same religion are all indicators of reduced or improper communication or a total breakdown of communication.

And it is the same within corporations. Human relations between colleagues or between bosses and subordinates can be considerably increased with the use of empathy and better communication. An excellent sense of humour, a humour shorn of all sarcasm, helps greatly to improve the quality of communication provided care is taken to ensure that **words make sense**.

Here are some examples of the gap between 'words' and 'sense':

The Pharmacy College in Ahmadabad was hosting a reception on behalf of the Gujarat University for an eminent lady, Miss Foster, the dean of an American university. The principal, Dr Patel, got up to give the welcome address to Miss Foster, a tall and stately lady well in her late-fifties. 'Everyone here knows that most of our students from the College of Pharmacy go abroad for further specialisation!' he said, 'The average for the last five years has been 80 per cent! And you all know that my relationship with my students is that of a father and son. In fact, Miss Foster, here, is the mother of my children in the US.' What he meant was quite different from what he said and what the audience understood. The packed hall with 500 students and faculty burst into peals of laughter. Miss Foster blushed in embarrassment. However, Dr Patel did not realise his faux pas. Finally, when the laughter died down, he carried on with the rest of the speech but no one listened. The bloomer had been made and now it was too late to retrieve the situation.

Often, in the corporate world, we do not say what we mean. Or having said what we mean, we are not understood in the manner that we want our listener to understand. There is, therefore, great merit in the old principle that we should count to five before we speak, and perhaps ask for a clarification, or count to 10 before we reply. Most of us fail to heed this warning. We begin by 'shooting from the hip' and, therefore, cause a problem *a la* Patel. Or, respond in a manner which is completely different from what we intend to mean.

Like the salesman who asked the prospective buyer's family, 'What do you want most to get out of your new car?'

(1) 'Good looks,' said the college-going daughter.
(2) 'Dependability,' replied Mom.
(3) 'My teenage son,' was Dad's answer.

Some of the responses we get are because the question asked is pointless in the first place. A silly question asked without thinking, elicits a silly answer. Like the truck driver who took a diversion because the road was being repaired and came to a bridge too low for his rig and got stuck. An onlooker came over and asked, 'Are you stuck?' The frustrated driver replied, 'No, I'm trying to deliver this bridge, but I can't find the address.'

Again, when a customer requested for a good book to read, the obliging librarian asked, 'Do you want something light or do you prefer heavier books?' 'It really doesn't matter', the reader answered, 'I have my car outside.'

There are so many cases of misunderstandings that books are full of funny stories, of how the receiver and the sender of the message are on completely different wavelengths. Like the boy who kept sniffing in the bus, which irritated a woman sitting nearby.

'Don't you have a handkerchief?' she asked him. 'Yes, ma'am', he answered politely, 'but I never lend it to strangers'.

Or, the story of the sergeant who asked, 'Your name corporal?' 'Robert Jones', came the answer. 'When you talk to me you say "Sir",' roared the sergeant, 'Let's try again. What's your name, corporal?' 'Sir Robert Jones!'

Or, the incident of the little boy who was following his father out of church when he noticed a series of plaques on the wall. When it was his turn to greet the pastor, he asked, 'Who are all these men?' The pastor said, 'Oh, they are men who died in service.' The puzzled boy responded, 'Was that at the 9 o'clock service or at the 10.30 service?'

Oscar Wilde was right when he ended a six-page letter with the apology, 'I would have written a shorter letter, darling, but I did not have the time.' It does appear contradictory. But it takes more time to write one page of good sense, tightly packed, than six pages of utter rubbish. And what goes for writing also goes for speaking.

A look at many reports and minutes within corporations, including the chairman's speech, and an analysis of a good deal of what is spoken in business conversation and at meetings will indicate that there is little thinking and planning before writing or, more often, before speaking. Indian mythology speaks about words which once spoken, like arrows, cannot be controlled or retrieved.

Therefore, the need to consciously follow all the rules, although to most of us they only seem sterile theory: **plan your communication, be on the same wavelength, say just enough, be brief, watch your tone, be precise, consider the total physical and emotional setting, remove all doubts, listen more than you talk, show benefits and get action and much more.**

It is important to remember that 'building bridges of communication' is different from 'repartee'. In a repartee, the receiver of the message fully understands it. In fact, so well that he can respond appropriately and fast. Winston Churchill was a master of the art. A lady Member of Parliament complained to him and said, 'Sir Winston, it annoys me to see that you always fall asleep when I speak in Parliament!' 'Lady Sandra,' replied Sir Winston, 'I fall asleep purely by choice.'

Or, on a more family-based note, the story of the well-known speaker who was invited to give a talk at an important convention. 'How was my speech? Did it go off well?' he asked his wife later. 'Yes, it was quite good. But you missed several good opportunities to stop and sit down,' she replied.

Communication is derived from the Latin communis. The word means 'sharing'. Communication is thus sharing of meaning. If this sharing does not take place, the receiver (decoder) of the message does not understand the sender (encoder) of the message. To make sense and to get results, we need to have communis. Do you understand?

26

TAKING NOTES
USEFUL BACKUP TO MEMORY

Shortcuts always cause problems.

—*PHILIP CROSBY*

One of the big sellers among business publications in recent years is *50 Rules to Keep a Client Happy*, published by Fred Poppe. This is a book every advertising executive should read. In fact, it is a book which everyone in any kind of service business, including management consultancy, should read. One of the chapters titled 'Notebook' starts with

I don't care how great a memory you have, you cannot hope to remember every single item in the myriad of details you have to retain in day-to-day account handling. This is especially so after a lapse of time. Keep a spiral-bound notebook. Date it daily and use it for keeping notes of meetings, phone calls, things that need taking care of and whatever. I've got files and notebooks that go back over a 10-year period. You won't believe how helpful they can be.[1]

---

[1] Poppe, Fred. 1988. *50 Rules to Keep a Client Happy*. USA: Harper Collins.

This is advice from a successful advertising executive and author, on what would seem to be obvious.

Sometime ago, a very eminent film producer was in India on a short visit. He was interviewed by some journalists. I was present at the interviews he had agreed to. There was one journalist who came prepared. He had his questions written down and in the right sequence. He asked for permission to use the Dictaphone and the permission was granted. In addition, he took some notes. He was with the expert for just 25 minutes. Yet, he produced an in-depth, serious, three-page article on the interview. The other journalist came unprepared, had a freewheeling conversation and did not take any notes. He said that he remembered everything, and that he had a photographic memory. He interviewed the producer for a full hour: it was an exclusive. And at the end of it he produced a one-page report. He had not sieved the material. He had forgotten much of it!

Many years ago, I used to rely on my own excellent memory (which I thought was excellent). I would interview five to six candidates through a full morning session. I would feel reluctant to take notes during the interview, lest it put candidates ill at ease or on guard. And to quicken the pace of progress, I would call in the candidates, one immediately after another.

When the last interview for the morning was over, after a quick snack lunch, I sat down to review the morning's work. I found that I could not recall clearly what happened at the first interview or the second. Where photographs were not attached to the application form, I could not even remember the faces of the candidates. Or if I did, I could not connect the face to the name!

The late Ian McKinnon, who was Managing Director of Glaxo India and a very successful executive, always passed on four bits of advice on interviewing candidates (and followed the advice himself). He said—be courteous to the candidate; let him do most of the talking; ask for his permission to take notes and take notes briefly and without losing too much eye contact. Some heeded this advice. Others did not, and ended up taking decisions which could have been better. McKinnon pulled me out of my own overconfidence.

Over 20 years, I have lost 20 per cent of my library of fairly carefully chosen books, painstakingly collected at some considerable expense. 'That seems an interesting book you have here. Have you finished with it?' I would admit that I had.

'May I quickly browse through it and return it within a few days?' 'Sure', and I would willingly give it. These are good friends who have a genuine interest in good books. Invariably the book never comes back. Very seldom do I remember, a week or more later, who borrowed which book. Or even, who the borrowers were in the first place.

It has taken me a long time to use a card box always kept near my library. I still lend books, but immediately enter the names of the book and the borrower on a card with the date and drop it in the box. It takes just two minutes to do this. But it ensures that the book comes back. The sheer act of making the note adds a touch of seriousness. The borrower knows I mean business. The book is generally promptly returned, even without a reminder.

I was awed and pleased to meet Dr Weinstein, the eminent professor of management at The European College of Management (INSEAD) near Paris. After we were introduced and finished the small talk, Professor Weinstein and I exchanged visiting cards. He looked at my card and then wrote the date, the place and by whom we were introduced, on it. Then he put the card in his pocket and continued the conversation. It taught me a lesson.

I have three large trays containing visiting cards, collected over the last 10 years. I review them now and then, generally under pressure when the number of cards become too much for the trays. Many times, on going through these cards, I cannot recall who the people are, where I met them and why I kept the card for so long. Had I followed Professor Weinstein's simple habit, I would perhaps have benefited greatly from the extensive contacts I have made, because I would then have been able to recall all the details which I cannot now.

I have seen many executives who return from a four-to-seven-day tour and then spend half a day trying to reconcile their expenses with the cash in hand. Invariably a gap seems to exist. Where did the balance money go? And if you cannot account for it, you have to pay for it. Every tour costs these executives, cumulatively, a good packet. After all, there is a limit to which an executive can remember the fares at six to eight taxi rides during the day, and all the snacks or drinks had at little stalls where you do not get a bill! Odd as it may seem, making notes at regular intervals, when the memory is still fresh, could save executives a lot of money—small amounts which cumulatively become of big value.

Of course, there are books on improving memory. There are personal training programmes that improve both mind control and memory. There are correspondence courses advertised in various dailies and magazines. And it is worth investing some time and effort in doing these courses.

Some years ago, I saw Mr Shroff give an exhibition of his phenomenal trained memory at a Rotary meeting, where 65 people were introduced to him. When the last introduction was over, he repeated all 65 names in the same sequence—accurately and without fumbling. He assured us that anyone could do it.

But even if we develop such prodigious powers of memory, with the diverse problems that every executive has to grapple with every day, it would still be a great help to develop the simple but critically important habit of making notes. The improved memory can then be used for facts which are worth retaining over a longer span of time. And making notes is now much more convenient with a palm or computer notebook.

27

BLOCKING COMMUNICATION
I KNOW IT ALREADY!

Words are what holds society together.

—STUART CHASE

The marketing director of the company had finished his presentation. His marketing team had put together a good plan for a new product with considerable potential for India, with an international brand name. The marketing director then threw the meeting open for discussion. Were there any comments, opinions or suggestions on what had been presented?

One of the directors suggested that since the product was a premium one, its price could be higher than what had been suggested in the presentation. The marketing director immediately responded that they had thought about it and, in fact, had decided to price it at the higher level than was now being suggested.

Another director suggested that for a product like this one, the focus should perhaps be on direct marketing, rather than on a mass media campaign. The marketing director immediately responded that they had thought about it and planned to put the emphasis on direct mail. The presentation had perhaps given the impression that the emphasis was on mass media, but it was not meant to be regarded this way! The marketing director asked if there were any other comments. There was silence all round. Since there was nothing further to discuss, the meeting came to an abrupt close.

Why had the meeting been a failure? Because the marketing director knew it already, and knew it all! There was nothing which was new to him. Everyone now felt that they could not possibly make any contribution after the presentation. He had better manage on his own and woe betide him if anything did go wrong with the implementation. All the others were only waiting for him to trip and fall. The marketing director had antagonised everybody with his attitude of 'I know it already'. It is the surest way to close the door to a dialogue or to a continuing communication.

I have known many salesmen who have ruined their customer–salesman relationship by hastening to show that 'they already knew' it all. When a doctor mentions to the medical representative that he has read about this new development in a past issue of *Lancet*, it is much better strategy for the representative to show admiration that the busy doctor finds time to read medical journals, and that he even reads foreign and expensive journals which are not normally current in India. The representative should further ask for details of the reference and some help.

Customers like to be in a position of power, in this case 'knowledge–power' than just the power to give an order. If, on the other hand, the rep immediately responds with, 'Yes, I know that doctor. It's in the February '93 issue of the *Lancet*,' then psychologically, the rep is bringing the doctor to his own level, and the customers' mental guards unconsciously go up.

The flames of many conversations at social occasions are fanned by pretending ignorance, by encouraging the friend to continue, by expressing surprise, by asking questions and seeking clarifications. Maybe you know a lot about it already. Perhaps you even know more than the person relating the story now knows. But if you pounce upon the first sentence with the retort, 'Oh yes, I knew it already,' you would have brought all party conversation to a grinding halt.

It is the same with children at home. There is so much they want to tell you about which you already know. It is their voyage of discovery. They are finding something new every day. It is an endless adventure. And they want to share it with you. They want to tell you what they have just found out—from a friend, from a book, from the teacher, maybe from just observation. 'Do you know how long the fireflies live, Daddy?' 'No, tell me'—and the whole strange world of wonder and pleasure, and of the joys of discovery, open out for this child. She rattles on and on, telling you what she knows, has heard or read. It would have been such a pity to say 'Yes my dear, I know it already.' It would be closing the door to an hour of fun, of companionship, of warmth.

A wise person, even when he/she knows a great deal of what is being discussed, listens attentively and carefully in an attempt to recheck if his/her facts are correct. It is useful to have multiple sources of information to confirm what you might already know. Or perhaps, fresh doubts could be raised. But if you get tempted to block the flow, to satisfy your ego and prove your superiority, then you miss such good opportunities.

Rushing into an 'I know it already' blurb can also be a source of great embarrassment. I was once at a dinner where someone remarked that dentists are now busier and making more mistakes as well. Sheela immediately interjected with 'Yes, I know' and went on to narrate a story of how a particular dentist pulled out the wrong and good tooth of her friend, and how most of her acquaintances in the area are now very reluctant to go to this dentist Raj for treatment. There was silence. Sheela wondered why. She asked the group whether anyone knew who she was talking about. 'Yes,' said a quiet, confident voice in the corner, 'I am the dentist Raj!' There was silence again.

There is the well-circulated story of the little girl who sat with her grandfather at the window seat of the train, describing to him in great detail everything that she saw in the rapidly passing landscape. The person in the next seat was getting irritated by the continuous chatter of the little girl. He could not concentrate on reading the newspaper. Why was the girl describing all this? Couldn't the old man see for himself? It was just then that they got up to get off at the next station. And he saw that the old man was blind. The little girl was 'seeing' for her grandfather. He had assumed 'he knew it already', and now he knew he was wrong!

It is said that the surest way to lose a friend is to tell him, 'You are wrong.' This method seldom fails. One could even reach a stage where there may be no one around left to be told, 'You are wrong.' On the reverse scale, the surest way to win a friend is to often pretend that you do not know what you perhaps do know. 'I knew it already' is a sure way of closing the door to a continuing communication. Unless it is a matter where it would be foolish to say you don't know, because you are expected to know it all.

28

COMMUNICATING FACTS WITHOUT TACT
YOU COULD BE RIGHT, THE WRONG WAY

A blow with words strikes deeper than a blow with a sword.

—*ROBERT BURTON*

It has been said that the surest way to make an enemy is to say to someone abruptly and brusquely—'You are wrong!' This technique seldom fails. It is so well proven that we need not even bother to test it.

But there is also a more sophisticated way of making enemies, and that is, to present facts without tact. Most of the time, these are facts that are totally irrelevant to the situation. But people raise or highlight these facts with a hidden agenda—to show the other person in a poor light, or in order to establish one's own superiority compared to others.

The manager today must be able to resist the temptation to climb the ladder of success by climbing on the backs of others. He/she must be able to set his/her own goals and have his/her own life objectives so that he/she does not measure his/her own progress in relation to others, but in relation to his/her own set goals. He/she will only make himself/herself more stressful and unhappy if he/she looks at his/her colleagues and the world with envy-tinted glasses.

I met Anil for the first time at the club. He was telling me that he had started a medium-sized engineering company in Pune and had just signed a foreign collaboration. The product he was making had a very high demand. He was lucky that he was able to make a fairly good profit in the first 12 months of operation. I congratulated him and wished him continued success. Just then, his elder brother who was also there (with many other common friends) and whom I had known well earlier, extracted himself from a conversation he was in and interrupted me. 'And do you know, Walter,' he said, 'He's done well even though he had failed in his O-levels, and got through only at the second attempt.' Anil tried to pooh-pooh this and move on with the conversation. But his brother Arun would not let the opportunity to belittle Anil pass off so easily. Arun added, 'Anil always stood seventh in the class in school. No one at home knew that there were only seven students in the class!' Anil agreed that this was in fact the case. There was some embarrassment all round. Arun had brought up a subject that was not material to the conversation. He tried to show Anil in a poor light. **He certainly related facts, but it was needless, and there was no tact.**

I met Shyam at a wedding reception. I knew him well, though our contacts were now infrequent. He was the managing director of a medium-sized company in Mumbai. When I was having a short social conversation with him, with crowds milling around, Kailash happened to pass by and stopped, 'Ah, how are you, Mr Vieira?' he said, and then, 'Hello, Shyam, how are you getting on?' Shyam said that he was fine. Kailash then shot his arrow, loud and clear for many around to hear. 'You know, Shyam was a typist in my typing pool 30 years ago. He's gone a long way since!' Kailash had no reason to go into all this. He was trying to find some ego satisfaction for himself, needlessly relating a fact without tact.

A little later, at the same reception, Shyam and I were again chatting when Gita came up to us to say hello. Gita had been working in a company where Shyam and I both worked for some years and therefore, we both knew her well. Gita introduced us to her husband, Mohan. I don't know what came over Shyam, because he did to Gita what Kailash had done to him a little earlier. In the presence of a large number of people most of whom were meeting Gita and Mohan for the first time, Shyam asked Gita, 'But were you not engaged to Robinder, when you were working in Perry's?' Gita blanched, then recovered to say that Shyam certainly had a good memory to remember what happened 15 years ago. Yes, she was engaged to Robinder but it had broken off. She and Mohan were married now for 10 years and had two children. Mohan tried to ignore the faux pas. Shyam's comment about this fact was without tact and completely unnecessary.

Persis and Jehangir had just entered and were being introduced to the other guests. Then they met Ravi who had known Jehangir since their school days. 'I am glad to see that Persis has lost a lot of weight, Jehangir,' said Ravi, 'The last time I met you both two years ago, she was beginning to look like a massive Amazon.' It was a completely tactless remark though perhaps a fact. Persis has been cold to Ravi ever since and Jehangir now keeps a distance.

My colleagues and I in our management consultancy company organise and conduct a large number of training workshops for corporate managers. Some people, like Dev, have the wrong impression that this is all that we do. Dev, who did a doctorate in chemistry at Cambridge and after many years as a production manager, finally 'arrived' as managing director of a small chemicals company, met me at a dinner party. I think deep down within himself, Dev feels he has not been compensated by progress in life for the investments he has made in long years abroad for his doctorate. So when I met him, he repeated his singular refrain for the nth time. 'You are certainly in a very happy position, Walter,' he said. 'You can earn your money by just being on your feet and talking!' What can you say to someone who presumes that all clients are fools who will pay anyone for the gift of the gab? His problem was that he was seething with envy of others who had achieved more, with perhaps less investment in academic input. This will always happen. Once again, it was a fact, partly true, but needlessly stated, and without tact.

It is good for a manager to run his own race, without constantly looking over his shoulder. It is good to set your own goals and measure against these. Spouting forth even facts, needlessly and out of context, and further, without tact, can only help to build a wall around you, of people who may not wish you the very best.

29

Separating Issues from Persons
The Art of Discernment

Abuse of words has been the great instrument of sophistry, and chicanery,
of party faction, and division of society.

—*John Adams*

In standard books on the theory of selling, there would be three seemingly innocuous directions lost in the vast verbiage of a standard text, under the chapter on 'Closing of the Sale'. These are: (a) never be insulted by a refusal; (b) never write-off a customer and (c) never give up. It seems so obvious, that one wonders why they are mentioned at all! On reflection, I realise that both in sales and in life, we are guilty of often doing one of them and sometimes doing all three, with friends, acquaintances and customers. The one that I am tempted to focus on is the first, 'Never be insulted by a refusal.'

Ramesh was known to my friend Anil for a long time. Ramesh was one of those who worked for a large private sector company and just about managed to keep his clerk-level job over 28 years. Most of the time, however, he spent in selling life insurance. He was absent from his seat for much of the day, but this was hardly noticed. This was quite an achievement! In fairness to Ramesh, he provided good service to his insurance clientele. He maintained individual files, sent his own reminders for payment of premia and suggested changes in the insurance portfolio. Anil was very happy with Ramesh. Four years ago, Ramesh had some serious family problems. His service levels fell. Some of his clients, including Anil, moved to other insurance agents. Ramesh took this as a personal insult and began to quarrel with Anil and others. He no longer even speaks to Anil.

Ravi was the son of a friend and colleague of my father. He had applied for a job advertised by my company. He seemed to pass the preliminary criteria and was called for an interview. Soon after the call letter was sent out Ravi's father phoned my father to tell him that Ravi was to be interviewed and he hoped that I would do my best to help him. Ravi appeared for the interview on the appointed day. He came in late. He asked if he could smoke, despite the 'No Smoking' sign on my desk. His body posture seemed defiant. His knowledge levels for this particular assignment were poor. With many other better candidates available, Ravi was not selected. Years later, Ravi is cold in his manner, whenever we meet and our paths cross. His father never spoke to my father after this incident. Ravi and his father took Ravi's non-selection as a personal insult.

Suresh had been moved to the Jubilee Nursing Home in Mumbai. He was in a serious condition with a kidney problem. Suresh's wife was distressed. She thought of the worst that could happen with three children, all under 12 years old. She got one of Mumbai's well-known urologists to operate on Suresh. It was expensive, but she was taking no chances. She wanted the best. Of course, she had known that her neighbour's son, Roy, was also a urologist. He had graduated from the UK and returned to practice in India last year. He was still in the process of settling down. Roy's parents were very upset. How could Mrs Suresh get someone else to operate when Roy was available? And a neighbour too! This was a personal insult to a neighbour and Roy's professional competence! Roy's family and Suresh's family still live in the same building, but they have not spoken to each other since that surgical operation on Suresh.

Mrs Patel was a social worker involved with many causes. In fact, she was a worker in search of a cause! From starving children to the helpless aged, lepers and cancer patients, famine and flood relief—you name it and Mrs Patel was associated with it.

When I worked as marketing manager of a multinational corporation, Mrs Patel would approach me every two months with a request for an advertisement in a souvenir being brought out by one of these organisations. When we could afford it, the ads were released. Then came a downturn in the market. We cut our 'optional' advertising budget. We had to say 'No' to Mrs Patel. The first time she took the refusal graciously. I explained the market situation and said, 'We would have, if we could, as we had done in the past.' The second time, a few months later, she was not as understanding. She seemed visibly annoyed to the point of rudeness. She has been cold and distant ever since. She has taken the refusal as a personal insult!

Ram's auditors and accountants were Vinay and Associates. Vinay was an old and close friend of Ram over 20 years. However, in this association, both Ram and Vinay had taken precautions to be absolutely professional. Ram paid the standard market rates for the service and expected no concessions. Vinay was always asked to raise bills for extra services as and when required. However, Vinay did not do this. Over a period of 15 years, Ram's business increased and so did Vinay's. Vinay now had some large corporations as his clients and smaller clients like Ram were not getting quite the same attention as earlier. The result was that dealings between the two were becoming difficult, with Ram getting more and more dissatisfied with the service provided. Ram mentioned his unhappiness to Vinay on a few occasions. There were promises that all would be set right, more staff hired and personal attention given. But it never happened! After three years, Ram sent a letter discontinuing the association and changed over to another smaller firm which would have the time and expertise to give him better service. Vinay was furious. He sent a bill for services for which he claimed he had not charged for between seven and 10 years ago. And worse, he discontinued the friendship and refused to speak to Ram. Vinay had taken Ram's withdrawal as a personal insult rather than as a discontinuation of a professional association. These examples are a rule rather than exceptions.

This happens to most of us. We refuse to distinguish that someone or anyone has a right to say 'No' to an offer of a product, a service or a favour. The 'No' is not a rejection of the person who is making the offer. The two must be separated. We need to learn to do this with facility and ease.

30

DITHERING ON DECISIONS
A MAJOR DISABILITY WITH MANY

'What is truth?' said jesting Pilate—and would not wait for an answer.
—FRANCIS BACON

One of the hallmarks of a good executive and an effective leader is the ability to take decisions. If they are usually the right decisions, he/she would be considered to have done an excellent job and would be regarded as a good executive.

However, most of us suffer from a 'fear to decide' complex. We get cold feet with the anticipation that our decision may turn out wrong, and that we may have to pay a very heavy price for it. We forget that we may have to pay an even heavier price for not taking a decision at all. All decisions are fraught with risk. The greatest of leaders can, and do, take decisions shown to be wrong after the event—Napoleon attacking Russia in winter, Hitler doing the same, Churchill and the battle at Galipoli, John Kennedy and the Bay of Pigs, the rescue of American hostages from Iran—the list is endless. There is much to be learnt from studying the decisions of such leaders. In the executive manual, there are four categories of poor decision makers.

(1) Those who **do not take a decision** at all. They prevaricate, dodge and try to escape responsibility by blaming others or the environment, for not being able to take decisions.

(2) Those who **get others to take decisions**, which rightly should have been taken by them. They will then take credit if it proves right, and pass on the blame if it goes wrong.

(3) Those who **sit on the fence** and keep changing decisions ever so frequently and changing their mind with every new influence that they came under.

(4) Those who **delay taking decisions**; and when finally they take one, it becomes irrelevant in the changed situation.

Shyam was the CEO of a small multinational in India. He became CEO at 42 years of age and had a stint of 18 years before he retired. The company was in India for 40 years and grew to just ₹150 million during this time. While multinationals such as ITC Ltd found ways and means to expand despite hurdles such as the Monopolies and Trade Restrictive Practices (MRTP) Act as well as the Foreign Exchange Regulation Act (FERA), Shyam found shelter under various excuses such as government policies on equity, new products, and on corporate headquarter's attitudes. 'It is not worth growing', he would often repeat. And the best and most ambitious managers kept leaving him over a period of time, seeing no possibility of growth—for the company and for themselves. Shyam dodged taking a positive decision. He escaped responsibility by blaming others for not being able to decide.

Prakash, another CEO, was under pressure to reduce losses. Input costs had gone up substantially, but selling prices could not be changed because of government price controls. He agreed with his marketing manager Gopal that one of the ways open to them was to reduce the numbers of the field force. They both agreed that all those who had been recruited recently and had yet to be confirmed could be discontinued. This could bring in substantial savings. Gopal went ahead and implemented the decision over the next month. There was an uproar and the labour union protested strongly on behalf of the discontinued field force. The CEO walked away from the scene. He had nothing to do with the decision. It was Gopal's idea. Gopal had created the problem by implementing an ill-advised decision!

And how many of us have met the likes of Raj? He was in the market for a computer system to improve the MIS of his medium-sized company. He would seemingly 'finally decide' on a different source every week, depending on which selling team was the latest to see him to convince him of the merits of their own product.

Bala was the commercial director of a large company in Mumbai many years ago. He had called us in to do a study of distribution systems and distribution costs for a certain range of consumer products. We would have long meetings, late into the evening. We would then give a proposal. Bala would promise to study it. And we would not hear from him for six to eight months. Then he would call us again. He would change the parameters. Another set of long meetings would be held, another proposal submitted, another 'hatching' period of six to eight months. Then he would change his mind again! We never went back after the third time.

Decision making goes well beyond the executive office. Beware of the executive colleague who accepts your invitation to lunch and then parries your question of 'What will you have?' with 'Anything is fine with me!' He would seem to be a poor decision maker and it is possible this trait would extend back to the executive floor.

On the other hand, there are those who have a clarity of goals, who use all the information they can get, then weigh pros and cons (often writing them down) and arrive at a decision. There are those who reduce the element of emotion and increase the content of the rational, who know that in taking a decision they have acted sensibly and well, and are now prepared to take the risk even if things go wrong.

31

How to Motivate People
And Keep Them Motivated

What I do best is share my enthusiasm.
— *Bill Gates, CEO, Microsoft*

An executive or a manager will generally have a team of people to work with. He/she will be the leader of the team. Therefore, **he/she needs the ability to get people to do what he/she wants done to achieve the company's objectives**. In other words, as a leader of a team, he/she needs the **ability to motivate**. If he/she has this ability, it could make up for many other weaknesses. If he/she does not have this ability, it could negate many of his/her other strengths.

There are those who motivate with the weapon of fear. This can work for some time and with some people. What we are really looking for is the ability to motivate without fear or favour—to get people to do their work because it has to be done, and because they love their job.

Prem worked for a multinational, where it was known that not many people, especially in the sales department, lasted beyond seven years. The company seemed to believe that salesmen beyond 30 years of age had gone over the hump. But the philosophy of 'work hard and achieve, or you will be out sooner or later' (generally sooner than later!) permeated the whole organisation. The chief executive was a terror. Employees and executives tried to have little to do with him. A call from him to meet him was most unwelcome. Many in the executive cadre suffered from stress-related diseases and there was always an electric current of tension in the air. Looking back now, Prem reflects how happy they all were when the chief executive retired. And he also knows how lonely his former boss is. He has no friends. He commands no respect as a person. He was only considered 'somebody' because he carried a designation, and the designation gave him the power to mete out criticism or praise (rarely), and the power to hire and fire.

But most of us are looking for a leader who can motivate without the awesome power of fear. A leader who is one of us, and yet not one of us; who we regard as a friend and yet who draws the line between friendship and familiarity; who trusts but is not naive; who is fair and also seen to be fair.

Given below are some of the qualities such a person would have:

(1) A good motivator sets **a good example**. He is the role model. He preaches through his actions, rather than through sermons. He is the sales director who at least sometimes visits the marketplace, gets wet in the rain or scorched in the sun, who dares to visit the difficult customer and the rural market which may not have a two-star hotel. Or he's the production manager who often moves around the factory floor.

(2) The good motivator is **quick to give recognition**—for an asset that may have been developed or an achievement by one of his men. And not just private recognition, but a public acknowledgement that says 'thank you' in the presence of peers.

(3) He ensures **involvement by building enthusiasm** within the team for achieving a common and shared goal. He makes each one, no matter how big or small the person is, a partner in the enterprise. And with such involvement, the good motivator ensures participation so that everyone carries a part of the burden.

(4) He **does not stint on praise**. He is generous with it, though he does not give it as charity. He ensures that his praise does not come cheap. It is only given when well deserved, and consequently it is a matter of rightful pride to the receiver. Such praise is tied up with recognition and can be encapsulated in those five most important words—I am proud of you! So easy to say, yet rarely said.

(5) A good motivator **eliminates the tendency to boss**. He uses 'we' rather than 'I'. **He shares credit and praise**. And when things go wrong, he takes a major part of the blame. He is never the boss; he is always accepted as the leader.

(6) A good motivator **dispenses rewards according to performance**, not personality. He cannot be accused of favouritism. His only measure is, 'How has he done compared to the objectives set?'

It is easy to talk and write about motivation. It is so difficult to come across executives who are real motivators. Often, they may not be found at the top of the management pyramid. They may be there, among the crowd of sales supervisors and production foremen. Their greatest reward is that their people enjoy every moment of working with them and will remember them long after they have left the group for greener pastures. Often, people working under a motivator say, 'What I am today is because of that person.'

A friend of mine says the same about his mother. He used to stammer and was a below-average student. All his five brothers and sisters were exceptionally brilliant. But his mother kept motivating Sunil, encouraging him to enter public speaking contests, consoling him when he lost, and encouraging him to try again until he bloomed into an unusual adult. Today, he is a senior executive at the International Monetary Fund in USA. Whoever thought he would have made it that far? Not even he! But his mother had the courage, the patience and the faith. She was a motivator!

32

THE NEED FOR CREATIVITY
BECAUSE INNOVATION IS THE KEY

*There is rarely a creative man who does not have to pay a high price
for the divine spark of his 'Great Gifts'.*
—CARL GUSTAV JUNG, 1930

It is a turbulent world. A world of change and chaos. All the time,
I see that old solutions which I had successfully applied to problems 25 years ago are no longer suitable for the same problems.
This is compounded by the fact that even the basic nature of many
problems has changed. Hark back to the old dictum that 'the only
permanent feature of the marketplace is change'!

This marketplace does not respect the status quo. When I
started my working life at Glaxo in the early 1960s, if we introduced a new product, we were certain that we would get a five to
10 year monopoly run on it. Betnovate retained a monopoly for
a long time, and so did Grisovin. This is no longer true. When
Glaxo marketed Zinetac in the 1990s, the product was in fact
preceded by imitations. Glaxo did not even have the privilege (as
original inventors) of being the first of the pack. A classic case of
how times have changed!

This is why in most enlightened companies, top management
is looking not just for efficiency, or effectiveness, but also for

creativity. That uncommon ability to look for new solutions to old problems, to look for different solutions to new problems, and to look for possible solutions to problems that may arise later and which a good manager can generally foresee.

The petrol gauge of my car was not working. I thought that the petrol tank was full when, in fact, it was nearly empty. Mercifully, for me, the car came to a grinding halt at Sion (Mumbai) and close enough to a large petrol pump. I parked the car, fished out a can from the boot and walked to the pump with my then 12-year-old son, Samir. Only when the attendant had filled in four litres did I realise that the bottom of the can had a crack and therefore a leak. Could the attendant lend me a can? No. Could I buy one? No. I was at my wits' end when Samir suggested, 'Why don't you cap the can tight and then hold it upside-down till we walk to the car?' So obvious once you've heard it! It was a creative solution and that's what we did.

For many years I saw a single call button for a battery of four lifts in the large hotels. When you pressed the call button, you would have two or sometimes three lifts coming up at the same time, responding to one call. This continued to happen until someone used a 'creative spark' to programme lifts in such a manner that only one of the four lifts, closest to the floor that called, would move to respond to the call, thus saving a lot of energy and expense. When you look around, you will see many examples of creative thinking, but unfortunately not enough; and not as much as is needed to solve today's problems. The seemingly simple development of a pencil with an eraser attached, developed by Hyman Lippman, to the car with a radar which would pick out the easiest route between two points, to the TV which can be fitted on the wall to save floor space, to the washing machine which can wash clothes (without detergents) only with ultrasonic waves. And the once simple refrigerator, which was just an icebox with electrical power, now has four doors, spouts for cold water and ice, and separate sections for soft drinks.

There is the machine developed to generate electricity from rice husks; the litmus strip specially treated to test saliva for diagnosing tuberculosis; the use of glass instead of steel in orthopaedics (and developed by an 18-year-old girl); the battery operated scan machine for use in rural areas which have no electricity; and the list is endless.

Sam Swaminathan, writing in *Gulf News*, lists five myths about creativity.

One, that creativity is artistic talent. Yes, artists need to be creative. But they are generally not creative outside their own field. Business is perhaps the only field where people are required to be creative in a variety of situations.

A second myth is that creativity is synonymous with intelligence. It is not. Intelligence is inherited. What we do with it depends on our thinking, i.e. our creativity. You can have a monkey driving a Jaguar car, or a highly-skilled driver at the wheel of a '48 Morris. The latter would fare much better—because he brings thinking (creativity) into the process. The former would probably drive the Jaguar into the nearest lamppost.

A third myth is that creativity is dependent on analytical skills. It is not. The right brain deals with creativity and ideas. The left brain handles analytical skills. The ability to evaluate alternatives has nothing to do with the generation of alternatives. Without creativity, you cannot get new ideas. Analysis helps judgement; creativity helps exploration. We need to suspend judgement in order to explore.

A fourth myth is that creative people are crazy. This is because creative people appear to be crazy compared to those who are 'uncreative', because creative people seem to do things differently. Creativity is as serious an activity as logical thinking.

A fifth myth is that creativity cannot be taught. That people are born creative, they cannot become creative. But thinking is like driving and can be taught. It is not just an allocation of intelligence that you are born with.

Remember the story of the simple factory worker on the packing line who suggested that the size of the nozzle of the toothpaste tube be increased by 2 mm? He was creative. After the suggestion was implemented, far more toothpaste flowed out—and more profit flowed in.

Creativity is one aspect of thinking. Many universities such as Durham in the UK offer courses in creative thinking. And the crying need for creative thinking is being felt in all companies around the globe—by those who are unsuccessful and those who want to remain successful.

Very few in top management are doing anything substantial in nurturing creativity. They will invest in the latest technology, forgetting that new technology is available to every one of their competitors. Those who buy a few months later, buy the latest and the best, and so it goes. The real lever of success is the people who create the technology. That is the intellectual capital of the corporation. It is what makes managing people so important in today's context. It is your people that can bring to the company their creativity, their commitment and their thinking ability. This will make the big difference between corporations that succeed and those which fall by the wayside.

In a jocular way, survival today needs the creative genius of the three Scotsmen who did not want to respond to the loud and earnest plea for an additional generous contribution to charities, after the first collection in the Church service they were attending. They had already contributed the first time earlier. As the collection tray approached close to the group there was a certain embarrassment—until one of them fainted and the other two carried him out.

The right brain had taken over!!

33

LEARNING FROM JOB TRANSFERS
TRAVEL IS EDUCATION

All mankind is divided into three classes: those that are immovable,
those that are movable, and those that move.

—*AN ARAB PROVERB*

I have met very few people who were actually excited about job transfers. People like to stay in one place, grow roots, spread branches. They like to build friendships, to belong to a neighbourhood, and to be part of a community. The thought of uprooting; packing all belongings into wooden and cardboard boxes; being forced to review what they really need and don't; to throw away what they don't immediately need; to throw away some things that may be totally useless in a utilitarian concept but very precious as sentiment—can be very painful.

It does help of course if you belong to a family that has often or even sometimes been transferred. If your father was in the Railways, and shunted from Gorakhpur to Kharagpur, or from Bina to Jhansi or from Secunderabad to Doleswaram, every three years, then you are used to it. Or, if he was in the Air Force, with postings in Jodhpur and Hakimpet; or in the Army with postings at Jalandhar or Dehradun, Pune or Chennai. He could be in the central government services, or the Indian Administrative Services

(IAS), or the more colourful meanderings of an IFS officer. All this means being psychologically prepared to travel at short notice, or getting immune to it in a boarding school by going to a different destination during the holidays every two or three years.

Even with such a background, there is no insurance. It is possible that you have travelled or been on transfers for many years, but would now like to 'settle down'. Either the wife is complaining or she wants to pursue a career, or you want to be in one place so that the whole family can be together on at least some basis of 'permanence'.

However, you may be in a situation where transfers are a part of the system. You have no choice and might as well enjoy it.

The **first step is** *acceptance*. You have to accept the fact that transfers in your job are inevitable. If you're in the IAS, IFS, revenue services, armed forces, an all-India marketing organisation or a corporation with many factories, then you must know that there will be transfers. Otherwise you should have joined the Bombay Port Trust—in the knowledge that the job will be at a port, and a port cannot shift.

The **second step is a** *positive attitude*. You have to remember that transfers will probably give you a promotion in status and emoluments, that they are all steps leading to your ultimate goal. That with every transfer, you will increase your experiences and interactions and become a more experienced person, better equipped to handle a variety of problems.

The **third step is to have a sense of** *realism*. So arrangements have to be made for schooling of children (perhaps boarding school), for temporary pursuits of a career by the wife (teaching or a small business), for maintaining personal and nonpersonal contacts with close relatives and friends, having hobbies and interests that do not demand the need for an anchor.

The **fourth step is to have or develop a sense of** *vigorousness*. There are people who have lived on the same street for 30 years and do not know each other. There are others who have lived in the same building, perhaps even in apartments on the same floor, and also do not know one another. This is not altogether a good thing, but these people can afford this luxury because they will still have many other friends, having lived in the same town for decades. The person who is being often transferred, however, needs to develop new friends in the new location. He/she needs to develop these friendships quickly. There is not much time. In another three years he/she will be gone somewhere else and he/she must keep in touch with at least some of the friends he/she made in locations he/she has been in the past. This will help him/her to keep socially active and spend his/her leisure pleasurably.

The **fifth step is to develop a sense of *togetherness***—if this is possible. In many cases, it is. In some cases, it is not. If you are in the armed forces, the IAS or the Railways, you will meet others of similar circumstances and avocation in your new location. This is a great help and consolation. You can immediately get into the 'stream of things' and the transition is much smoother.

There are some who tell me that they would not like to live in the same building or colony with others from the same company. They would not like to get restricted to 'the same crowd' in business as well as socially. A period of 40 years may be too long a period of 'togetherness'. But for two to four years, there is little likelihood of familiarity breeding contempt, or of prying, interference and consequent unhappiness all around.

The **sixth step is to develop an abiding *interest in people***, in customs and in surroundings. This genuine interest will change your whole personality. It will make you less critical of every new location, new neighbours, new club. And as much as you show interest in people, they will show interest in you. Liking is generally reciprocal and you will get as much as you give.

To say that these are steps, one following another, would not be quite right. These are generally simultaneous stages and concurrent attitudes. However, you may have all these attitudes and yet not enjoy or look forward to transfers. Your child may be in the critical years of school and any disturbance/interruption might cost a 'career'; you or your wife may need the kind of medical treatment which is possible in Mumbai but not in Sholapur; you may have an old parent who needs attention and care, and cannot be moved to a new location; you may need to arrange a daughter's or sister's marriage; you may be in the middle of a three-year part-time, learning programme. It can be one of so many reasons.

But one thing is sure. If it is possible, do get around. Travel is education. Living with and in the midst of different kinds of people with habits, styles, cultures different from your own can help to broaden your vision, lower barriers, make you and your children better human beings; and in your career, make you a better, more complete executive!

34

PERSEVERANCE PAYS
IN THE LONG RUN

In the confrontation between the stream and the rock, the stream always wins—not through strength, but through perseverance.

—*ANONYMOUS*

Shashi came to me just one and a half years after I had selected him as group product manager for a large consumer durables company in Mumbai. He was not happy. 'What happened?' I asked him. 'I am not making much progress,' he said. 'I have been here already for over a year and I see no way in which I can become the marketing manager within the next two years.' 'But what is the hurry?' I asked him. 'Well, most of those who were in the batch of '88 at management college have now become marketing managers of small or big companies; while I have been left behind! It is expected that an MBA will become a marketing manager at least six years after he has graduated—or he is just not good enough.'

Sitting there, looking at Shashi, I wondered if the present generation of managers has lost the capacity for dogged perseverance. Have we come to the quick-fix age? The age of instant gratification or tantrums if such gratification is not achieved! This used to be true in the past for some children in their formative years. But had this now developed into a general norm with young adults, especially those who have been privileged with specialised higher education and belong to the class of 1988? Will the likes of Shashi, who do not seem to have the staying power, ever be able to build up large and growing businesses in an increasingly competitive environment?

My mind went back to the story of Walchand Hirachand, the founder of the Walchand Group. When Hirachand decided to set up an aeronautics factory (which was later nationalised and is now known as Hindustan Aeronautics Limited), he went to the UK to negotiate with Hawker-Siddely for the engines. He was kept waiting by the managing director for two whole days and then told that the MD would not have the time to meet Hirachand because he had to fly to the US the next day. Most of us would have thrown up our hands in disgust, thought poorly of the company and its pompous managing director, and returned home. But not Hirachand. He found out the name of the airline and the flight number and got a first class seat next to the HS MD. On this long transatlantic flight, they got talking and had a chance to informally discuss Hirachand's proposal. By the end of the trip, they had become well acquainted and agreed to do business. Hirachand's dogged persistence had paid off!

When G.D. Birla set up the Hindustan Aluminium Company (Hindalco) in 1962 at the behest of Jawaharlal Nehru who was very keen at the time on the industrial development of Uttar Pradesh, he had been promised electricity at a certain concessional rate from the Uttar Pradesh State Electricity Board (UPSEB). This was a big incentive because electricity constitutes a large input in the manufacture of aluminium. Some years later, UPSEB broke the agreement and unilaterally raised the tariff. Hindalco could have complained till they were blue in the face. They could have rued the day they decided to build the plant relying on the assurances of a government or a state body. But G.D. Birla looked at the situation as a pointer to a direction and a lesson to be learnt. Against all opposing views within the company, he decided to set up his own power generating unit to supply power to Hindalco.

He carried on doggedly. Today, Hindalco is a successful, profitable operation with a captive power plant which has among the highest generation efficiencies in the country. Men like G.D. Birla did not give up so easily. They made things happen.

I am told that Jamshedji Tata used to gather some friends on an occasional weekend and organise picnics to Khandala during the monsoon. One of his great pleasures was to see the gushing waterfalls on the *Ghats* in full fury after a good monsoon. He would have a distant look in his eyes. He would tell his friends that in Switzerland he had seen electricity being generated from water power and that he would like to do this in Khandala. Most of his friends would dismiss these comments as the fantasies of a 'dreamer'. But Jamshedji Tata was not one to just 'watch things happen'. He 'made it happen' and so the Tata Electric Company was born—a pioneering Indian effort to generate electricity.

Further away is the oft-repeated story of an American who finally became president. He failed in his school exams; his college exams; he failed to get into a career he wanted. He failed at elections to the Senate. But he tried again and again and again. Until Abraham Lincoln finally became the President of the United States of America.

All this might have been many years ago. But some recent examples include John Hamilton of Cargill Seeds, with its headquarters in Bangalore. With the kind of protests that Cargill has had to face from the Karnataka Farmers' Union and the physical damage inflicted on their office and property, the natural reaction would have been to quit and leave. But not Cargill and not Hamilton. He dug his heels in and didn't budge. Today, persistence has paid off.

Dhirubhai Ambani, starting life as a gas station attendant in Aden, went on, with sheer persistence, to build the biggest corporate empire in India within just 30 years. Dhirubhai had the vision, the creativity, the boldness and the persistence to 'make things happen'.

Some lessons are timeless. These are especially for the quick-gratification generation that we may now be producing. Like the story from Greek mythology of Prometheus who was ordained to cross the Aegean Sea in an earthen pitcher. An accident with a rock would mean the end of the journey. Like Prometheus, managers are called upon to reflect both on vigilance and persistence, if they are to successfully cross their own Aegean corporate sea.

PART THREE

Attitudes and Values

The manager's speech and actions will reflect his deep-rooted attitudes and values, in the same way as the sea reflects the colour of the sky. The student of managerial style will, therefore, have to be discerning to relate one to the other.

35

Is Business Etiquette Outdated?
These Are Lubricants that Help Human Interactions

We meet on the broad pathway of good faith and goodwill; no advantage shall be taken on either side, but all shall be openness and love.
—WILLIAM PEN

Whenever one talks about business etiquette, the response is generally 'tepid'. Many will tell me that business etiquette is a Western concept. In countries like India, we, need not take it seriously. We don't have to ape or abide by Western norms. We are fine as we are. The others had better accept us just as we are, or they can just forget it. And yet, if India is going to make any dent in international markets, Indians will have to take business etiquette seriously—both the general business etiquette as practised internationally, and the refinements in business etiquette that are applicable to specific geographical areas.

I read a report some years ago that said that the Japanese spend over $20 million in a year in business etiquette training programmes. They are investing time and money because they know that this is a necessity. While most may know that the Japanese have conquered the world in terms of economy—with innovative products, higher quality, lower cost, etc.—few realise that they have taken the trouble to back up this hardware with fully trained personnel. Not just trained in technical skills, but also in business protocol, to help smoothen the tortuous course of business in distant and strange foreign lands.

We will never be able to quantify how much business has been lost in the international market because of lack of knowledge of business etiquette. Nor will we ever know exactly how much has been gained. Business etiquette knows no national boundaries. **By definition, business etiquette is acting in a manner that shows consideration for others.** Can there be anything wrong with that? Or can such a philosophy be the monopoly of any country or any one segment of the world?

The elements of good business etiquette are:

(1) Be punctual
(2) Be discreet
(3) Be courteous, pleasant and positive
(4) Show concern for others rather than just yourself
(5) Dress appropriately
(6) Use proper spoken and written language

To expand on the above elements:

Being on time to keep an appointment is an important prerequisite in business etiquette. It is worth keeping aside 20 per cent extra time to take care of contingencies (more than required for travel, etc.) so that we will not proffer lame excuses such as 'The traffic was horrendous this morning' or 'I missed the earlier train'. My own experience has shown that the busier the person in life, the more punctual he/she is.

Yet, when I was running a training programme for the staff of a national airline many years ago, many of the participants who were senior executives would wander into the room up to 10.30 a.m., when the workshop began at 9.30 a.m. It reflected on the kind of discipline that would exist in their own work situation. These were all senior managers who had large teams reporting to them. And if they were late every morning to attend a workshop which they had specifically come to attend from half-way across the world, then one could be nearly certain that this is what they did as a daily routine. Thus, they were setting a poor example to their subordinates and projecting a poor image to their customers. Over the last few decades, the financial and marketing performance of this airline has amply proved this forecast right.

In India, unfortunately, keeping people waiting is considered the 'form' by some in high places. It projects an image of being busy, of being submerged with work, of being important. An industrialist from Goa once rang me up and fixed an appointment to meet in Mumbai on a certain day a week later. He then rang up again one day before the date of the first appointment to change the date and postpone it by three days. I agreed to the next appointment and was at his office at 3.45 p.m. for the 4 p.m. appointment. I reminded the receptionist at 4 p.m. and again at 4.30 p.m. and was told that the managing director was busy. I finally left at 5 p.m. and never went back to meet him, in spite of two weak apologies later and requests for fixing a new date and time. From this first indication, I could only look forward to a long period of frustration and ill temper, arising out of this industrialist's poor business etiquette.

Being discreet is the second requirement of good business etiquette. A manager is a repository of many confidences. There are company confidences—new R&D projects, new products to be introduced, new organisation structures, impending promotions, new acquisitions and many others. Even more, there may be personal confidences—of family conflicts, of impending separations, of children on drugs, of an alcoholic spouse.

All this makes for interesting conversation. It gives a sense of power—a power that comes from knowledge. It is knowledge that others in the group do not possess. People love rumours and gossip. This explains the big sales of our film magazines. The large hoardings that advertise these magazines promise salacious news on the private life of Ms X or Mr Y. In this kind of environment, it is all the more necessary for us to be aware of the need for discretion.

It is said that most people discuss people; some discuss events; very few discuss ideas. However, those who discuss events and ideas are those who really observe 'business etiquette'. They are the ones who are discreet.

The third factor in business etiquette is to **be courteous, pleasant and positive**.

I was at the Mumbai airport, waiting in a queue for a taxi. It was 10 p.m. and all of us were tired and in a hurry to get home. One of those ahead of me was a foreigner. One of the passengers who had arrived by a later flight walked past us to the head of the queue, so that he could take a cab first. The foreigner called out to him to tell him that we were all in the queue. The policeman on duty belatedly did likewise. Much to my surprise this 'traveller by air' came back and stood at the end of the line and told the foreigner sarcastically, 'Thank you. Thank you, please go ahead!' When the foreigner got into the next cab, the ill-behaved traveller started shouting and waving 'Bye, Bye'. The foreigner ignored him. The rest of us were embarrassed.

Some years ago, three Hindi-speaking young men were in the London tube. They were speaking rapidly in Hindi and making some non-quotable comments about two attractive English girls sitting across the aisle. Occasionally, they threw glances in the direction of the girls. All went well for them until after about six stations, an elderly Englishman sitting next to the young men, got up to leave. Before he headed for the door, he stopped and told the young men in fluent Hindi, 'I wish you would not be so rude to talk about our girls in this fashion.' The young men were taken aback. The old man alighted. There was a deathly silence for the rest of the journey.

Courtesy and politeness pay all the time: during business hours, within the work environment and well beyond the work environment. Boorish behaviour, on the other hand, helps to tell people around, in a non-verbal way, where we come from and, perhaps, even where we are headed!

Another area of good business etiquette **is to show concern for others**, not just yourself. This is seen in the observance of queues for tickets, in giving a senior citizen a seat in the bus or train, in

opening the door for a lady, in not reaching out across the table
for the salt, in refraining from belching at the dining table, in not
jumping into a cab which has been hailed by someone else just
behind you, in not talking with your mouth full, in not smoking
despite the temptation to do so in an office with a 'No Smoking'
sign, in not taking a chair without being invited to do so and in
many such areas, too many to recount.

Some of these areas have no precedents and no standard response systems. However, each person's ability to be sensitive to
the needs of others always comes through with a certain transpar-
ency and shows that good business etiquette is being observed.

The secretary of our Rotary Club, who spent a lot of time on
Rotary activities, once told me that

> I never understand most of our club members. I phone in
> the morning and leave a message, because the person is in
> the bath. Most never ring back. Their argument is that if
> it is important enough, I will ring again. Why should they
> spend money in phoning back? It would seem that Rotary
> activities are only my private business.

I write to clients and friends—condolence letters in a bereave-
ment, cards on birthdays, greetings on special occasions. Some
will acknowledge and thank. Most never do so.

No return calls, no acknowledgement of greetings or letters are
all indicators of total self-centredness. A self-centredness which is
to the complete exclusion of the concerns and interests of those
around you. This is poor business etiquette.

The fifth requirement of business etiquette is to **dress appropriately**. There is a lot of controversy about what is 'appropriate'.
Jeans and Benetton shirts may be in fashion, but they are not office wear. Neither are sports shoes.

At the same time, one does not expect a sales manager, travelling with his salesman in Vijayawada in the summer with 47°C
temperature in the shade, to be in a suit and tie. A dark suit with
a sober tie would be appropriate business wear in England, while a
suit with a shine and a bright colourful tie will be acceptable in Italy.

Dress reflects the style, the attitude, the age, the class, the aspirations and ambitions of people. Dress must therefore reflect our personality and our values, and must also be responsive to the environment, the weather and the person who is to be met.

That is why a chairman of a company could be in a short-sleeved shirt but can still expect the sales engineer, calling on him from a computer company, to be in a tie or a safari. Your dress and appearance are part of your non-verbal communication, irrespective of whether you like it or not. In the way you dress, you make a statement about yourself; as did Jawaharlal Nehru's red rose, Mahatma Gandhi's loin cloth, Vinobha Bhave's and Arafat's headgear, Lady Diana's designer dresses, Mao Tse Tung coats or Jayalalitha's shoulder cape. When people contend that you are what you are, irrespective of what you wear and how you dress, this is not entirely true. Whether you like it or not, your dress and appearance make a 'statement' and tell the world around you whether you follow the rules of business protocol or not.

The sixth area of business etiquette is **using proper spoken and written language**. It seems so obvious, and yet is often flouted.

A 22-year-old computer programmer, out of a job, was sent to me by his uncle (whom I knew slightly), to enquire whether I could help with a placement. He came to the office, barged into my room and said, 'Walter, my uncle Mr X has sent me. He says that you will be able to find a job for me.'

The language was wrong. It was presumptuous of him to address me by my first name and then compound the problem with a statement, rather than a request.

Spoken language can facilitate or retard all interpersonal relationships. The most common errors are on the telephone. We do not answer with the name of the company or the phone number (if it's a residence), but with the commonly used vague 'Hello'. The tone of the voice is harsh and forbidding, with a further 'What?' instead of 'Pardon?'.

What does one do with written language—when the letter addressed to me displays the name of Balter Vora, or I am sent the fifth copy of a letter where the type is so unclear as to be totally illegible, or I receive Christmas cards with a totally illegible signature and my name not even written on the card? So we do not know to whom it is sent and by whom—and the whole exercise is a total waste of money!

Written communication also projects tone and empathy which are not restricted to verbal communication alone. Tone and empathy also need sensitivity, an appreciation of the attitudes and feelings of the receiver. Many managers believe that the use of Latin phraseology of 'Apropos your proposal of . . .' or 'Vide your letter of . . .' and jargon of 'Always at your service' will improve the tone of the letter. It doesn't. The tone and quality of the written communication will only improve by writing simply, correctly, directly and with politeness.

Business etiquette or business protocol will need to receive greater emphasis in the coming years as India becomes more and more a global player. It will be necessary not only to know how to play the game, but also the unwritten conventions of what is done and what is not done (especially what is not done at certain levels and in specific geographic areas).

As said earlier, the Japanese have taken the study of business etiquette very seriously. The trend is just beginning in India, with perhaps one or two companies pioneering this experiment. But by whatever methods this is done, a good knowledge of business etiquette will provide the required back up to the efforts that are being made to make a dent in global markets.

36

INDISCRETION CAN HARM OTHERS
HALLMARK OF POOR MANAGERS

For that is and ever will be, the best of sayings—That the useful is the noble and the hurtful is the base.

—PLATO, THE REPUBLIC

The ability to resist the temptation to declare 'I know it already!' is an ability to be discreet. Discretion is an important attribute for a manager, because carelessness and indiscretion in corporate life can do great harm to others and to the organisation.

Letitia Baldridge, the high priestess of business etiquette in the US**, lists discretion as one of the six cardinal rules of business etiquette. For whatever it is worth, it is listed as the second rule of good business etiquette, the first being punctuality!

At a time when the tabloids want to 'disclose all' about the various members of the British Royal family, when books appear on the shelves claiming to be authorised biographies of the rich and the famous or autobiographies written by ghost writers; when biographers claim to tell you 'the real truth for the first time', or when investigative books are published telling the story 'behind the story', then, perhaps, there is need to look again at the concept of 'discretion'.

An FBI agent recently told us what really happened when he was in the secret service. Princess Diana was helped by an author to spell out her predicament in an unhappy marriage. The former Indian President, Zail Singh, told us the story of his presidency. Mrs Sonia Gandhi gave vignettes of the life of her famous husband. And Pupul Jayakar gave an insight into the life of her close personal friend, Mrs Indira Gandhi.

It is a world of openness. A world of telling all, either before the event, during the event or after the event. Or so it would seem. And in this scenario, the executive has to reassess the environment. The executive is privy to many secrets—about company plans, research and development, financial arrangements and personnel. How much should he disclose and how and when?

Gopal was being interviewed for the position of marketing manager by the managing director (MD) of a pharmaceutical company. Sometime during the interview, when all the preliminaries were over and the in-depth interview had begun, the MD asked him what the sales were of a recently introduced product and the promotion budget. Gopal excused himself. He said he knew the figures, but could not disclose them. It was 'in company' information. The MD asked him what plans his present company had for new introductions in the next few years, considering the difficult economic climate. Again, Gopal said he could not answer him. The MD seemed visibly upset over such a 'non-disclosure attitude'. The interview ended on a pleasant note. But Gopal did not get the job. He had been discreet and it had not paid off.

On the other hand, Sam, in a similar situation at an interview, did tell the interviewer a good deal about his company's plans and recent achievements. All he needed was a little encouragement and he came out with all he knew. Sam did not get the job either. This MD felt that Sam would be as forthcoming with this company's secrets after he joined the organisation, as he was with the secrets of his present company.

Krishnan was distribution manager in the company where I worked, and reported to me. When I left the company to take on another assignment, Deepak took my place. My relations with colleagues in my old department were always cordial and continued that way, even when I met them later. However, I found only

Krishnan to be a little cold. Every time I met him (which was not often) the colder and more distant he seemed to be. One day I asked him directly whether something was wrong between us. Not surprisingly, he said yes. After I had left the company, Deepak had told Krishnan that he had gone through the personnel records and had found that Krishnan's promotion to commercial manager had been blocked because of my comments in the annual evaluation, and that now he (Deepak) would ensure that the situation was corrected. Deepak had thus tried to buy Krishnan's loyalty by being indiscreet about confidential personnel records.

Pradip was a people-oriented manager. His concern for people was even greater than his concern for the task. There was a time when the 'big boss' began applying pressure on Pradip to get rid of Joe, the advertising executive. Joe was perceived by the CEO to be inept and inefficient, in spite of Pradip's protestations. Pradip tried to help Joe by recommending him for two assignments in other companies which he knew were open and where Joe could qualify. Unfortunately, Joe did not make it at both places. He was disappointed and so was Pradip. But Joe decided to try another tack. He went and met the CEO one day and told him that Pradip said that the CEO was putting pressure on Pradip to terminate Joe. Joe told him that he had been sent for two interviews by Pradip. The CEO was furious. He did not want himself projected as the 'brute'. Pradip had been indiscreet by 'disclosing confidences'. Relations between the CEO and Pradip got very strained. A few months later Pradip was forced to leave the company. Joe stayed on for many years thereafter!

Raman, a salesman, was having a marital problem. He had to disclose this confidence to his colleague, the area sales manager because his problem was having an effect on his work and his sales. The colleague, Rao, fell into the usual temptation of showing off that he knew what others did not. He made some indiscreet remarks one evening at the sales conference dinner. Raman became the butt of pointed references and barbed jokes from many of his insensitive colleagues. Rao had betrayed a confidence and virtually ruined a career and a life.

Sanjay works in the R&D Department of a public sector unit. He has some friends who own chemical units, but do not have the wherewithal to conduct research. However, they are smart enough to know a direction from a minor lead. And Sanjay's seemingly small indiscretions cost the company heavily. The result is that new products and processes are being introduced in the market by these small companies much earlier than by the monolith that Sanjay works for! The public sector undertaking kept making increasing losses, while some of these smaller private companies kept growing, till some of them became large enterprises. The nimble footed companies profited from the massive inputs in research done by the PSU.

No wonder Ms Baldridge lists 'discretion' as a cardinal rule in business protocol. The executive is a repository of company plans, forecasts, industry data and personal confidences. He must be worthy of the title of manager by not being what in street parlance would be called a 'loud mouth'!

37

INDISCRETION CAN EVEN HARM YOU
SHOOTING YOURSELF IN THE FOOT

Let no man be sorry he has done good because others have done evil!
If a man has acted right, he has done well, though alone; if wrong,
the sanction of all mankind will not justify him.

—HENRY FIELDING

Many years ago, I admired Ramu who had rapidly moved from the position of salesman to marketing director with a large transnational company in Mumbai. He had achieved the pinnacle at just 34. It was a time when the chief executive was always an expatriate and, therefore, the appointment as marketing director was a high point for any Indian executive. Ramu moved into a large three-bedroom apartment on the Hill; he rode a chauffeur-driven imported car and enjoyed all the powers and privileges that went with his position in the company. His living style changed and he was the envy of all his peers.

Ramu's big dream came to a grinding halt one day, two years after he was promoted. The chief executive had the bad habit of swinging the door open without knocking and entering the offices of his senior executives. Early one afternoon, he went down the corridor and swung the door open to Ramu's office without knocking. And Ramu had his secretary on his lap, in a position not entirely in consonance with business protocol. Norbert, the CEO, did not say a word. He did not even betray surprise. He walked back to his room and phoned Ramu with a request that he come and see him. Immediately Ramu tried to give an explanation. Norbert raised a hand—it was all right, no explanations were needed. Very coolly, very deliberately, Norbert asked Ramu not to attend office from the next day. His accounts would be settled before he went home that evening.

Mel was the marketing director of a large multinational. He had earlier worked in another company as marketing manager for consumer products and had now moved to this prize assignment with the new company which had set up shop in India. The money and perks were good, and far more than what Mel was getting earlier. In fact, it was nearly double his earlier income. But the start-up job was tough, while the earlier assignment in an established company with well-known brand names was a cakewalk.

Two years later, Mel was still struggling to hold on to the job. He had returned from one of his visits to the Delhi branch of the company when a week later by coincidence, Sam, the Delhi branch manager visited the company headquarters at Bangalore. When Sam went to see the managing director, Lall, he chided Sam for not having treated the marketing director hospitably during his recent visit to Delhi. Sam asked Lall why he said that. 'Well', said Lall, 'the least I would have expected was that you keep the company car at the disposal of the marketing director, or any of the other senior managers when they visit the branch. This hospitality was not extended to Mel.' Sam insisted that the car and driver were at Mel's service all the four days he had spent in Delhi. Lall had just signed Mel's travel expense statement where he had charged for taxi hire for the four days. Mel got caught. There was no need for proof or for a confrontation. Lall quietly asked Mel to resign. Minor inadequacy on the job could be tolerated, but lack of integrity—never. It was just a matter of ₹2,000 but Mel paid a heavy price for it.

Marie Smith was the advertising manager of a large consumer products company 30 years ago. She was English, divorced, had been in India for 20 years and had worked with this company in India for just as long. She was in her mid-forties and to all of us in our early twenties she was 'over the hump' and 'old'. Roy was one of the four new management trainees and was doing the rounds of all the departments before being slotted to an area where he would specialise. At one point, 24-year-old Roy was posted in the advertising department. No one knew exactly when the spark of romance fanned into a full-blown fire. But when it happened and it became obvious to everyone that Marie and Roy were in love, nothing could stop tongues from wagging. Marie who had earlier been careless about her appearance was now well groomed.

They threw all caution to the winds and Roy moved into Marie's apartment. They arrived every morning at the office in Marie's chauffeur-driven car (to which she was entitled as a senior manager). Finally, the managing director decided that they could not both stay in the company. One of them had to quit. So she resigned her highly paid job and he gave up what seemed to be a promising career, to start a new life together in Australia. They had to pay for their indiscretion. I am told that the marriage could not bond a 25-year age gap easily and they broke up after just six years of marriage. It was a 'costly indiscretion'.

Shantu told me that when he joined a large conglomerate controlled by an orthodox family, he gave up drinking alcohol and smoking cigarettes. He also became a vegetarian. When he said this, my first response was that Shantu was over-reacting to the job change. A manager is expected to deliver, to give value for money, to make a contribution to the corporation. What he did in his private life was his own business. He could drink or smoke and it would not be of any concern to the employer.

Such was my view until I met Kuldip. He was the exact opposite of Shantu. He did believe that his private life was his own business, except that his private life spilled over into his business life. Kuldip had one too many at a party. It was all right until he reached a stage when he talked too loud, and worse, expected criticism of the top management and of the company (albeit jocularly) to be taken in the 'party spirit'. When Kuldip arrived with a 'few already under his belt' at 6.30 p.m. for a meeting with a prospective foreign collaborator in the lounge of a five-star hotel in New York, he was unsteady and fell back with the chair he sat on. There was a pregnant silence as everyone around watched. There was great embarrassment in this group of five, until Paul, the prospective collaborator, turned on the humour and remarked, 'I think Kuldip got the chair with three legs! It's not really his fault!' Four weeks later, I learnt that the collaboration never came through. Kuldip had projected the image of the company in a completely uncomplimentary way—an image of drunken stupor!

Jay was the chairman and managing director of a large, family conglomerate. He was doing well and signing up one collaboration after another. The conglomerate had grown five times in eight years since Jay had taken over from his father, when he was just 28.

But Jay had extended himself financially, and now with bank credit tightening up, he was feeling the pangs of rapid expansion. This was when Jay sought a meeting with the chairman of the Development Bank to make a case for a large financial aid package for a big project which was very important in the conglomerate's scheme of affairs. Jay went with Joe, the finance director. The meeting began on a cordial note. Jay had known Suren well, over many years. The conversation and discussions somehow got limited to a dialogue between Suren and Jay. Over a period of time, Joe's mind began wandering. Unconsciously he began rocking his chair with a vague look on his face. Suren tried to ignore this unacceptable behaviour for sometime. Then he lost his patience. 'It would seem that you are bored with what is going on, Mr Joe,' he said. The bite in the tone was not lost on any of those present. The discussions went on. One month later, Jay received a letter. The bank had turned down the request. And Jay wondered whether Joe was indirectly responsible for the bad news!

Indiscretions can be costly in the world of business. And perhaps even more so in public life. It can be illicit liaisons, money, genuine love that transcends hierarchies; addiction to alcohol or just lack of etiquette, because one did not know better.

In whatever form it comes, there is a heavy price to be paid.

38

A QUESTION OF TRUST
CREATES FOLLOWERS FOR LEADERS

It is an accepted fact that in the West, you first do business, and then build relationships—in the East, you have to first build Trust, and then, maybe, you will do business. Trust is the key to doing business, east of Suez.

In the old days, traders in India used to count diamonds, worth millions of rupees, and having accepted the count, just shake hands, and accept the result of the tally. Does this happen anymore? No. In the old days, diamond merchants would just put a 'lot' of diamonds in an envelope and send them from Surat to Bombay by 'angadia' (the Indian predecessor to DHL)—with full trust for value and delivery. Was there any problem? Seldom. It was Trust. Unless the train was held up by bandits (which was once in 500 years) the parcel would have been delivered. With no doubt!

And, therefore, diamond merchants trusted one another; all diamond merchants trusted the angadia services and customers trusted the final sellers of diamonds from the showroom.

Does this work any longer? Yes and No. Unfortunately in a world of changing values, it is becoming more 'No' than 'Yes.'

How do you develop Trust? How do you know that the person you are dealing with is trustworthy? Many Japanese, Europeans, Americans are concerned about the Trust—Index of Indians. Just as they are of the Trust Index of Individuals and companies in many other countries!

A director of a company to whom I was a consultant, many years ago—was a good man (Jose) a technical expert; made a contribution to the business and every Sunday, spent time at this Church. He hosted the breakfast after the 8 a.m. service for 200 people who attended the service. The snacks and coffee was supplied by the cafeteria of the company of which he was a director. He had not taken official permission for the supply. The owners of the company were Hindus who were kind enough to pay for the breakfast after a Christian ritual. But Jose was really taking from Peter to pay Paul. If he was honest—truly honest—he would have paid for this supply from his 'personal' funds. But he was cheating and the owners/directors knew this and overlooked this. However, Jose lost trust of the directors and everyone else who knew. Yes, it was charity—but Jose was working out charity at his company's expense rather than on his own. And the directors and staff who knew about this, lost 'Trust' on this simple and uncomplicated matter.

When I was a sales manager with Warner—I took an unscheduled personal visit to Belgaum. At the Belgaum train station, I accidentally met the Warner Medical Representative for Belgaum getting out of a II Class compartment and moving towards the exit. Warner MRs were paid I Class fare to travel—so that they can travel in comfort and rest; and do a good job on the working day after. Shyam, was obviously cheating the company and travelling II Class, when charging I Class fares in the expense statement. For many years, I had held Shyam in high esteem. At the Belgaum station—I lost this; because I found he was not honest. I had lost Trust.

Trust is a strange and difficult to describe, concept. Easy to specify. Very difficult to fulfill. Trust is a one-mistake game. Very seldom you have a second chance. Either you are trustworthy or you are not. Westerners will do business, sign contracts and continue long-term relationships, as they keep building trust. In the East, they want to first build Trust, and only then they will do business. That is why it takes longer to work out contracts/ affiliation in the East.

At the beginning of your career you have to decide—are you going to build a career based on Trust? Or are you going to join the ranks. If you want the India of tomorrow to join the ranks of New Zealand, Singapore, Finland and Sweden rather than remaining at the bottom 20 out of 170 nations—then you know what you must do!

39

KEEPING YOUR WORD
IS BEING TRUE TO YOURSELF

*A man who seeks truth and loves it, must be reckoned precious
to any human society.*

—FREDRICK II THE GREAT

Some weeks ago, I picked up a simple but effective publication called *Life's Little Instructions,* and it taught a simple lesson life teaches us to keep our word.

When I was in my teens, I remember my father telling me that in some business communities, a 'word' was sacred. If a 'word' was not kept, it would be considered a most grievous sin; not just by the person who had been wronged, but also by the entire business community. A person who did not keep his/her word would be ostracised. He/she would find it very difficult to even exist in that commercial environment, because everyone he/she would need to deal with, would have mentally labelled him/her as 'not trustworthy'. It was therefore accepted that members of these communities could be accused of many wrongdoings, but seldom of not keeping 'their word' in business.

Many years later, I visited the Bombay Stock Exchange and saw how stockbrokers used a code of signs to indicate buy or sell, and to indicate prices. These signs were accepted by the 'receiver' of the message, and there was never a situation where the 'sender' later said that he meant sell and not buy, or that the figures he had communicated were wrongly interpreted. The **sign was a word, and it was sacred**. If brokers went back on what they had actually said, the whole stock market would be in disarray and no business would be transacted. Everyone would have been at their computers, to keep sending confirmatory memos!

However, in the wide, wide world outside the stock exchange, and outside these special communities, the 'word' no longer seems to be considered sacred. How often we meet friends and say, 'We must have you over'. I catch myself doing this, and then with a heavy travel schedule and other commitments, fail to keep my word.

I met Sheela once again at a dinner the other day. She is an acquaintance I have known for over 20 years. Once again, for the nth time, she said, 'Walter, I must have you over some time. I've been meaning to do this for so long. Let me give you a ring next week after I fix a date. Are you in town for some time now?' I assured her I was going to be in town for the next two months and that I was looking forward to hearing from her. But I knew I would not. Sheela has never kept her word. She had said the same thing before and had never meant what she said. Was it likely that Sheela used this gambit only as good social conversation or as a 'hook' to ask for a lift home, after the dinner?

At a beach hotel in Bali some time ago, Tanku, the manager of the hotel, came around one morning while I was sitting outside our cottage. He gave me a lot of information on Bali and offered to accompany my wife and I on a sightseeing tour the next day. We went round seeing the ancient Hindu temples and Lake Batur, and many other sights. Before we parted, he said that we were very lucky to be in Bali at the time of the biggest festival of the year on eighth and ninth September. He said that we must visit his house on the eighth and see how the Balinese celebrate the 'Christmas' of Bali in their homes and their temples. We waited the whole day for Tanku. He was also on leave from the eighth to the 11th. And when we left Bali on the 10th of September, we did not meet him to find out what happened. He had not even phoned. Although it was a small matter, I felt hurt that Tanku had not kept his word. Like Sheela in Mumbai, for Tanku in Bali, perhaps 'the word' did not mean anything.

We became acquainted with a German couple in Bali and decided to share expenses and go together to see the 'temple in the sea', near Denpasar. Handrich rented a car and drove us to Denpasar, where we both went our separate ways, to see the museum and other places of interest. We promised to meet at 4 p.m. and then go to the temple because Handrich had read in the brochure that the temple looked glorious at sunset. After that, he said, we could all go and have a meal at a restaurant he had heard about. We met at 4 p.m. at the appointed place. Handrich said that Ilka, his wife, was not feeling too well, and could we please drive straight back to the hotel? He said that they had already gone to the temple on the sea, and it was not as impressive as he had hoped. He consoled us by saying that we had not missed much. How did Handrich decide to go to the temple without us? Were we not supposed to go together? There was not even a mention of why he had not kept his 'word'. After all, he was literally in the driver's seat!

I thought back to even written contracts in business, that are sometimes not honoured. A drilling equipment company in Bangalore asked our consulting company to do an investigative study. The proposal was submitted. The fees were agreed to. The agreement was signed. Half of the fee was paid in advance. The study was completed and the client satisfied. And the balance did not come despite numerous reminders. Then the chairman wrote, asking that the balance fee be waived, because he now felt that the amount already paid was adequate remuneration to the consultancy company. He was not prepared to honour even the 'written word' of his company.

When I arrived at the Mumbai airport, I took a taxi home. The policeman on duty took down my name and address at Chembur. This is a deterrent to errant cab drivers, who only want passengers on a long haul, going in the direction convenient to the drivers. So when we reached the half-way mark at Sion, the reluctant cab driver who wanted to go in the opposite direction, insisted that he would proceed no further. I could take my luggage and go—after paying the fare, of course! I objected. He became rude, obnoxious and began shouting. Finally, I relented. Another cab came alongside. Would he go to Chembur? I asked. Yes, he said. When I reached home, I asked him how much the fare was. He said he would not charge. The trip was free. Why? Because his colleague in the profession had not kept his word. He had seen what had happened. 'It was a shame on the taxi driver community,' he said. He wanted to make amends. He was keeping the word, on behalf of his colleague, even though he did not know him personally!

Keeping your word, is building your character. It gives you self esteem, and a sense of self dignity. In modern parlance, you build a 'brand', which you can be rightly proud of. In that process, it is also good for all those around you, and who have to deal with you. They can all 'rely' on you, because you are dependable. You keep your word.

40

Building Credibility
Helps Create Reputations

Truth, whether in or out of fashion, is the measure of knowledge,
and the business of the understanding.

—John Locke

Keeping your word, in spite of difficulties or changed circumstances, helps to build trust—and trust in turn builds
credibility. Credibility is what gives substance to individuals and
corporations. At a time when so many newly set-up companies,
especially in plantations and non-banking finance, have cheated
gullible investors, it may be worth reflecting on 'building credibility'!

Some months ago, I was going on a business trip from Mumbai
to Frankfurt. I took a Lufthansa flight at 2 a.m. and was scheduled
to be in Frankfurt by 7 a.m. local time, to be able to start work at
9.30. I got into the aircraft and promptly dropped off to sleep. I
woke up a few hours later and looked out of the window. I imag-
ined the aircraft was on terra firma. I was confused. From what
I knew, this was a non-stop flight from Bombay to Frankfurt. I
asked my neighbour if we had made an unscheduled landing en
route. No, he assured me. We had not yet left Bombay. There was
a technical snag and the pilot refused to fly the plane unless the

matter was set right. We were now scheduled to take off at 5.30 in the morning.

For me, Lufthansa meant 'punctuality'. It was an image they had created and projected—and backed up by performance. On these rare occasions that the flight was delayed, I was prepared to excuse them. Because they had built up their credibility over many years—an image of which they could justifiably be proud.

Thirty years ago, I worked in some of the southern cities of India. I had a lot to do with transportation and distribution. And it was always said all over the south, that you could check the time on your watch with the passing of the TVS goods carrier. TVS was punctual up to the minute. I do not know whether this is still true, but at that time, TVS had very high credibility.

In his video film *Passion for Excellence,* Tom Peters talks about Federal Express, one of the most consumer-oriented companies in the world. And he gives the example of a FedEx courier who could not get messages through because a telephone wire had snapped after a snowstorm. This young man hired a helicopter, waded through knee-deep snow and against all odds, made sure that he refixed the telephone lines so that messages could go through. He was imbued with the FedEx spirit. He did not wait for permissions or delegation. He created the authority for himself, so that FedEx was able to maintain credibility with its customers. And remain true to the FedEx promise of 'delivering every time, on time'.

Rank Films has an excellent film on salesmanship, called *Starting the Interview,* and director Ian Latimer makes the comment that customers look for four characteristics in a salesman, and the first among them is credibility. He gives examples of salesmen making exaggerated claims and using words such as 'works miracles', 'astounding success' and 'complete breakthrough' which put customers off and project the salesman as unreliable and possibly even as an outright 'liar'. On the other hand, it helps to build credibility when the salesman (even one who sells an excellent product) at best offers to help, with perhaps the possibility of success.

There is then the flip-side of the coin. I once missed the Air Canada flight from London to Mumbai. I arrived at the airport a little too late at 10 a.m. and was in a flap because I had to reach Mumbai the following day. The Air Canada counter staff were, sympathetic. 'Try Air India,' someone said. 'They have a flight scheduled at 9 a.m. It comes in from New York and goes to Mumbai.' She saw the surprise on my face as I looked at my watch. Then she added, 'They are generally late and always have room!' I was initially angry that she had spoken so badly of our national airline. I went to the Air India counter. Yes, the flight was five hours late; and there was room. For once I was glad that it was so. But it also showed me that Air India lacked credibility, and suffered in the process.

There were two gentlemen from Sweden travelling with me on the early morning flight from Mumbai to Bangalore. We got talking. 'How did you like Mumbai?' I asked. 'Well, we arrived late last night from Stockholm,' one said. 'Well, you will like Bangalore,' I said. 'We leave back for Mumbai tonight', he informed. 'Then you will have a chance to see Mumbai on the way back,' I told him. 'We leave tonight from Mumbai to Sweden.' I was surprised. They had travelled all the way just to spend a day in Bangalore. It transpired that they had placed a large purchase order for leather garments from a company in Bangalore. They had liked the samples and the price was right. They had now come to check that the factory actually exists, with the machinery and the personnel. Why two of them? So that they can pinch each other and reconfirm to themselves that it is really true! Was this necessary? They said it was. Five years earlier, they had placed an order with a company from Delhi. They had approved the samples, accepted the price and paid an advance. The stocks did not arrive at the appointed time, or even a month later. When they sent a person to track down the company, they found an automobile garage operating at the address. They had never heard of this garment company. This Swedish company had a very poor opinion of the credibility of Indian suppliers.

I was associated with a company marketing consumer durables, a business where the retail distribution is very important. The company had 200 stockists for the last eight years. With an increasing range of products and increasing volumes of total business, it was necessary to increase the number of stockists to at least 300.

Every year, for four years, the marketing director made an annual presentation where he showed plans to increase the number to 250. And every year, the review of performance showed that 10 stockists had quit and 15 had been recruited, with a net gain of five. After two years, the Board just took the marketing director's estimates and projections with the contempt they deserved. After four years, the marketing director was no longer on the assignment. He had lost credibility, with his superiors and with his peers.

Vinay, who headed a large industrial empire, was a very benevolent president. He hated to take any action against any employee, especially if it was for inefficiency. He could be pushed into acting with a firm hand only in cases of proven dishonesty with money. Vinay had somehow forgotten that the basic foundation of good motivation is good discipline. That employees do not mind a tough boss, provided he is fair. The result—the empire was getting peopled by poor performers in key positions and the company was sinking. When Vinay reprimanded anyone strongly for non-performance, they knew that he would not carry out the threat. There was no credibility to the tough postures he occasionally took.

Credibility is what gives substance to individuals and to the corporation. Credibility requires a matching of profession and practice. Credibility is helped by the adoption of strong postures—the absence of tall claims and false promises. Credibility is built over a long period of time, because it is a part of character. And like good reputation, although credibility takes years to build; a few months or just one incident can destroy it.

41

Making and Breaking of Reputations The Long and Short of It

My friend Homi, told me that his father the late and legendary C.H. Bhabha, who was one of the most reputed bankers of yore, kept dinning into the children **that there were only two things worth accumulating in life—education and reputation. Both of these cannot be stolen from you.** Both take a long time to accumulate but can be easily and quickly lost. Here was a moneyman talking—**and he did not put the emphasis on accumulating money.** Homi told me that he, likewise, tries to instill these values in his children. Will they succeed in a world where established reputations are being broken every month, sometimes, every week?

In recent times, there has been news of Mr Dominique Strauss-Kahn, who was the head of the International Monetary Fund, and was intending to contest for the President of France. He was accused by a hotel maid in New York and had to appear in court for improper behaviour. He had risen in the hierarchy over many decades, and within a few weeks, he was a 'hounded celebrity'—both in the USA and in France; and in fact, throughout the world.

There is Tiger Woods, an icon in the sports world- and the uncrowned King of Golf. He got caught out for infidelity, had a marital problem, which then affected his game, and more, his high reputation. It was a reputation he had built over a decade and it took just a few weeks to completely destroy it. The repair process has begun, but it is going to take a long, long, time!!

There is Bernard Madoff, the supremo of Ponzi schemes in the world, who became a billionaire, building castles for millions of people—till it was found that these were castles built on sand. He was finally caught out—and ended with a 125 year jail sentence, which can only mean 'death in Jail' since he is well into his seventies!!

And there is our own Rajat Gupta—the brilliant and very personable young man, who won scholarships to work his way through IIT and Harvard and then joined McKinsey to become the first Asian to head the most reputed consultancy firm in the world. He even made it to the Indian Prime Minister Advisory Council, and helped to set up the Indian School of Business in Hyderabad. Finally, he was accused of insider trading—and in a few months he lost a reputation he had built over 40 years. A reputation built, without money, influence or pedigree, but just by his own brilliance.

One is inclined to ask: What is it that makes intelligent, successful people like these, throw a dice and risk their solidly built reputation?

Is it overconfidence? Is it arrogance? Is it loss of judgement? One will never know the motivation. It is enough to know that all of us have to be careful—and to know that it takes decades to build a reputation, and a few hours or even, minutes, to destroy it.

It is like seeing the Taj Mahal monument on fire!

42

PEER GROUP PRESSURES
CAN BE OVERPOWERING

It has never been as much in the past, as it is now. And perhaps, it will be even more in the future. The peer pressure on the individual, of the peer group. If you do not fall in line with the group, you could get isolated; left out; considered a quirk; a stick in the mud. And 'not one of us'!

That is how a young person gets initiated into smoking—to be one of the boys! Or drinking alcohol till one is totally drunk and unstable—'to be one of the girls.' Or taking to 'ecstasy'—to be 'one of the hep crowd.'

In Mumbai, we have had so many examples in recent years. Of a young man who packed his car with friends after a drunken party—and drove recklessly down the sea side promenade late in the night, to finally drive over some labourers sleeping on the pavement, killing some and injuring the others. A few in the car had not drunk at all. But they were 'part of the group'. And they got implicated.

There was the big party at the beach side restobar, which was raided by the police. And most of the young people arrested, who came from wealthy homes, were tested positive for 'drugs'. There were also some here, who claimed that they did not partake. But they got implicated—because they were part of the group. Peer pressure had brought them here—and there was only trouble at the end of the tunnel!

The first value in **Charles Vance's** book *Manager Today, Executive Tomorrow* is '**You are alone**' in life.[1] You are really the master of your own destiny. You can make or you can break. You may have parents to help you on in the early part of life; friends and classmates and teachers, later in life. Even later there may be the spouse and perhaps children. They are all there as companions and as resource, for some of the time, at different times in life. No one in your entire life can really help you, except as a **temporary** 'aide.' The reality is that **all** the time, we are **all alone**.

We must, therefore, strike our own path and clear the way to create that path. No one else can do this for you. **You are alone!** We all are. Finding solutions in 'group movement' to identify **your** life's goals, is a dream, a chimera. You have to write your own life script. And the script is different, for every individual.

But if you can be with the crowd and yet not a part of it. If you can stand aside, with your own beliefs, and goals and time schedules to achieve them, you will win in the long run. There may be transient embarrassments and even jeering. But if you know where you are going—it will not matter. You will get there. Many of them, may not.

Its like the motorist who whizzed past you by overtaking from the left, then zipped through traffic changing lanes and going beyond speed limits—and who you see meeting with an accident further down the road. You are not glad it happened. But it did.

And you keep driving along at a steady pace, following the rule book, to finally reach your destination.

[1] Vance, Charles C. 1974. *Manager Today, Executive Tomorrow*. USA: Mc Graw Hill Book Company.

43

THE LIMITS OF HONESTY
CHALLENGE OF BLACK AND WHITE AND SHADES OF GREY

It is said that truth is often eclipsed but never extinguished.
—TITUS LIVIUS LIVY

The ability to be discreet, to build trust in yourself and through you, in the organisation; to keep your word, and therefore, to build credibility, can make big demands on an executive. Is it possible to always be honest? Are all issues always black and white? What are the grey areas? It may be worth reflecting on the limits of honesty.

Vita Engineering Company seemed to be having a lot of quality problems. When the marketing manager spoke to the quality control manager, the latter dismissed these customer complaints with a wave of the hand. 'Our products,' he said, 'meet the ISI standards. If customers want quality beyond that, they can go elsewhere. For us, the cost of creating quality higher than the bare minimum is disproportionate to the extra sales we can get. We only promise "good quality", not "extraordinary quality"!' And so there was a stalemate between marketing on one side, and production and quality control on the other. It was a borderline case of an honest claim, which needed more thought.

To many people in the corporate world, problems of integrity seem to be such borderline cases. Fewer cases are clearly black and white. A very senior personnel manager told me that an executive selection company had offered him a commission (or kickback) on all business he could give to the selection company. He asked the person soliciting his custom to leave his office and never come back again. Although one can use the argument that the whole world is now corrupt and such a solicitation is nothing unusual, it is still a case of black and white. Accepting a bribe is wrong and although one may try to explain it away, it cannot be morally justified.

However, there are many situations, which are not so clear. They seem to be the grey areas of corporate life. And most of us are guilty of taking advantage of these grey areas at one time or another. For example:

(1) In New York, my friend Raj asked me whether I would like to communicate a message to my family in Mumbai. I said, 'Yes, I will go to the telephone booth and do that some time during the day.' He said that if the message was not very personal, he could do that for me, easily and for free. He could always ring up from the insurance company where he worked. In fact, he rings up his family at least twice a week. In an organisation of that size, he said, it just does not matter. These are small expenses and no one seems to care. 'They all do it,' he said. This last statement justified the means. So should I have said, 'Yes?'

(2) Arvind was at the photocopying machine early one morning before the office started at 9.30 a.m. He seemed to be immersed in getting some photocopying done and had a whole pile which he had already completed. It seemed very unusual for Arvind to be at work so early; in fact, he had a reputation for being invariably late. I asked him what he was busy with. He said that his son had wanted parts of a book photocopied and so he had brought it to the office to get it done!

(3) Rohit was on a trip with me to Bangalore. We were going to attend a conference there for two days. We were going

by the morning flight and returning to Mumbai the following evening. Yet, Rohit was carrying a suitcase which had to be checked in. I thought it strange that he should be carrying so much luggage, for just two days' stay. A small bag would have been enough! It was much later that I found out that Rohit had all his clothes dry-cleaned only when he went on business tours. He seldom spent money of his own to get this done. In his perception, it was an acceptable 'travel expense'.

(4) Anil wrote to me every month, ever since he was transferred to the Delhi branch of his company. He liked to keep in touch with his old friends. The fault was ours that we never reciprocated in the same manner and with the same frequency. But that apart, it seemed odd that Anil always used company stationery for all his personal correspondence, and it seemed that he used office postage as well. An indicator—the envelopes were franked rather than with postage stamps, as would normally be the case with envelopes posted by an individual.

(5) A five-star hotel group has a well-worded warning in their hotels. 'There is a beautiful white bathrobe provided in the hotel room. It is available for your use. Should you wish to take this bathrobe home, please inform housekeeping who will arrange a piece for you on payment of ₹350.' Too many bathrobes had disappeared into guests' luggage from these five-star rooms. Hotel guests who paid over ₹5,000 per night were not expected to take away bathrobes and slippers provided for use during their stay. But they did. To directly state that bathrobes should not be stolen would be brusque. So the warning was couched in a phrase with an offer to sell a piece to those desiring them.

(6) The medical representative of a large multinational pharmaceutical company travels by second class but charges the company the first class fare, which he is eligible for. He has done this for so long that he has now come to believe that the difference in the two fares is a monthly allowance justifiably due to him because of the rigours of

outdoor work and long periods of stay on tour. The company had allowed first class fare so that the salesman could travel in comfort and be fresh and enthusiastic for his day's work. This purpose was not being served. With every increase in the first class fares by the Railways, the salesman's side-income increased and he was jubilant. When the company imposed a regulation that henceforth all representatives must attach a railway voucher or ticket with their expense statement, the salesmen's union went on strike. They felt this new regulation was 'unfair'.

Many will admit that a five-star hotel does not get much poorer with the loss of a bathrobe or a towel, or a large corporation with some additional expenditure on postage, stationery, telephone calls or fax charges. These are very small items of expenditure which will contribute to neither big profits nor big losses. So isn't it wise to turn the Nelson's eye to such goings-on and only concentrate on the large-scale frauds? In the end, each one of us has to make our own decisions.

But we must always remember that corporate misgovernance, begins with these little sparks, and before we know what has happened, they blow up into giant and all consuming flames. This is how the numbers increase in the procession led by Enron—to the shame of industry, auditors and governments.

44

TOLERANCE FOR CORRUPTION
GETTING USED TO SEEING WEEDS, NOT FLOWERS

We all live under the same sky, but we don't all have the same horizon.
—KONRAD ADENAUER, 1876–1967

Most executives feel that it is fine to talk about trust, credibility, honesty and issues in 'black and white'. But when it comes to living and delivering results, you cannot ignore the garden patch which is full of weeds instead of flowers. This is the environment of corruption in which we have to exist and deliver.

Sometime in 1995, the magazine *Fortune* published what was called an 'Asia Corrupt-o-meter'—a corruption barometer for Asian countries. This is a guide for American companies seeking to do business in Asia, who face a nightmarish legal dilemma. The attractive emerging markets for foreign investors are also the most corrupt. This was a report of Political and Economic Risk Consultancy (PERC), a Hong Kong-based firm that analyses corruption and political stability in different countries.

China, Indonesia and India were rated the most corrupt, with scores of 7.31, 7.00 and 6.59, respectively. Japan and Singapore, with 1.97 and 1.19, were rated the least corrupt. It is a consolation for us in India that we are not rated the most corrupt. It is a further consolation that corruption exists everywhere, however little, even in what is regarded as the most 'aseptic' country in the world; if this is any consolation at all!

And what does PERC suggest? Learn how the system works and cultivate local leaders without giving questionable payments. This is easier said than done, especially when competitors show up with briefcases full of cash. And most local leaders do not welcome visitors who do not carry a heavy briefcase!!

Many of us in these countries have got used to the idea. We know that if we don't pay a 'tip' to the telephone repairman, he will not show up the next time we need him. In fact, the telephone linesman in our area now walks with a strut, with neighbours nodding a greeting as he passes, as if he were the governor of the place. We know that the municipal inspector will not have the accumulated garbage of three days collected and removed, unless he is paid a 'tip'.

Years ago, when I went for a sales tax registration and needed a form to fill up an application, the peon said he had run out of them. Then I saw him performing the trick of producing an application for those who slipped in a ₹10 note. These forms were to be given free. They were applications for registration, so that one could pay tax to the government. Should one then give a tenner and be done with it? Or file a complaint and spend a lot more money making a few trips to the commercial tax office? Most people choose the easier route.

Again, a few years ago, the Inspector for Shops and Establishments visited the office of a friend. He asked for the records, as he was to do. He found minor faults and blew their importance out of all proportion. Ajay decided he would pay nuisance prevention money, because this was what the inspector was hinting at. He put ₹250 in an envelope and passed it on to the Inspector, who promptly opened it and counted the amount. With a sneer he returned the envelope. 'You know, Mr Ajay,' he said, 'even the peon in our department would expect more than this.' The unstated had been expressed. Both the intent and the amount! What should Ajay do?

It was like the old story of the waiter in the restaurant who returned the tip to the customer with, 'Thank you very much, Sir, but I think you need it more than I do!'

And so it goes. From the political rulers of the country to the humble peon in the commercial hierarchy. Those who have chosen to tread the straight and narrow path are a minority, perhaps even a fractional minority. For the many whose conscience has not yet been deadened and who still wish to distinguish between the completely right and the totally wrong, an ethic has evolved where being righteous means not accepting bribes. But giving bribes is a different matter, because one cannot survive otherwise. One would have to close shop!

This attitude of 'acceptance' was beautifully encapsulated in the opening remarks of the delegate from Indonesia at an Asia Pacific Conference Investment Conference at Kuala Lumpur, which I attended. 'Ladies and Gentlemen,' he said, 'for many years we have heard the boast that Britannia rules the waves. That may no longer be true. But it is still true that in Indonesia, we waive the rules. So come and invest in Indonesia.' The audience burst into laughter. But he had made a point. He had also demonstrated a helpless acceptance of the situation as it is.

Gaby Mendoza, former Chairman of AIM Manila and, in my view, one of the most original and interesting management thinkers in Asia, once wrote an article in the now defunct *World Executive Digest*, entitled 'The Judgement of Hermes'.

Mendoza asks, how do you convince bright young men and women that honesty and integrity are important attributes of the successful businessman when, even before they step out from school into the 'real' world, they hear of nothing but the shady deals and corrupt practices that big businessmen engage in and get away with? When all around them, they see well-connected men accumulating great wealth, not by producing honest goods or useful services, but by peddling their influence and looting the public treasury?

Mendoza says that men who are careful with their money are not highly regarded in Southeast Asia. We look down on them as tightwads. We like a man who knows how to spend money, who is lavish with it, who generously dispenses it as if there were no end to his wealth. And as many of us as can act like this, do so. We tend to regard resources not as something we should husband the use of and conserve, but as something to spend and expend.

Mendoza adds that frugality as a virtue, is not a Southeast Asian concept. It is an intrusion from the dour west, beaten into shape by the wintry parsimony of Calvinistic parsons fulminating against pleasure and wasteful living. It is an alien injection into our value system. And it has not taken root. The immune mechanism of our societies' soul has rejected it forcibly.

Gaby Mendoza further explains that it is ironic that most present-day accounts of the Sisyphus legend depict the hero as someone being wrongly punished. In the original story, Sisyphus was a conman who tried 'to pull a fast one' on the gods of the underworld. When his time came to die, he instructed his wife not to pay his funeral honours. As soon as he arrived in Hades, he bitterly complained of his wife's neglect and obtained permission to return to life in order to properly chastise her. Once restored to life, however, he refused to return to the underworld as he had promised. It was Hermes, whose job it was to accompany the souls of the dead to the underworld, who imposed the punishment of eternal frustration on Sisyphus for his deception. It comes as no surprise to find out, therefore, that Hermes was also the Greek god of business, a pursuit that requires continuing confidence and trust in one another if it is to endure.

Mendoza also believes that there is an insidious spirit that dwells in most of us in the developing countries of Southeast Asia. It is a spirit that tempts us to take shortcuts; to risk all on the turn of a card, the fall of the dice; to resort to get-rich-quick schemes. It lulls us into indolence, lures us into mindless ostentation, and leads us into deception and dishonesty. It is a spirit which, unless exorcised by a basic change in our values—a realisation that the radical virtues of hard work, frugality and honesty must henceforth shape our lives and our future—will condemn us and our people, worthy sons of Sisyphus, to remain ever more 'the hewers of wood and the carriers of water' for the more ambitious, the more assiduous, the more industrious countries that surround us.

Gaby Mendoza could not have used stronger language and given a more severe indictment of the state of society in our part of the world. There are not too many parts of the world that have been left untouched.

There was a very big scam unearthed in India many years ago and was aptly labelled the *Hawala Jain scandal*. It involved the illicit transfer of money abroad to, generally to tax havens. It opened a *Pandoras box*, and we all thought that a cleansing process in the government had started. And that in turn, it will spill over into a cleansing process in commerce and industry, and our whole social fabric. It did not happen. Perhaps, things have gone worse.

We await the Messiah!

45

GIFTS: GIVING AND RECEIVING
MAKING IT INNOCUOUS, BOTH WAYS

I fear the Greeks even when they bring gifts.

—*VIRGIL*

At Christmas some years ago, my boss received a hamper from one of our stockists. It had fruits, chocolates, dry fruit and nuts and four bottles of Scotch whisky. He kept the fruit and the chocolates, but returned the whisky with a polite note that the company did not allow him to accept such expensive gifts and, therefore, he had to return them, although he was most grateful for the kindness and the thought.

Many years later, in another company, one of our stockists sent a gift of a silver salver with six silver glasses to my house. My wife did not accept the parcel. The stockist was upset. It was the silver jubilee of his company and he was giving the same gift to all his business associates. He said that after 25 years, he could well afford to distribute a gift of such value, and the value was 'not much' to him. I also found out that my own boss and colleagues had accepted the gift, and my refusal was causing considerable embarrassment to them, especially to my boss. He began making sarcastic comments at the lunch table about the 'high moral principles of some among us'. I found that the best and most honourable way out was to accept the silver set.

My friend Soman, who was materials manager with a very large corporation, lunched out at five-star hotels three to four days a week. Suppliers vied with one another to entertain him and he gave them all the pleasure. So each supplier would have the pleasure of his company perhaps once in five months, which was not much at all. And so he justifiably carried on with this well-ordered schedule.

There is probably no other area fraught with so much confusion as the business practice of giving and receiving gifts. Yet, when the motives are clearly the fostering of goodwill and relationship building, rather than a manipulation of influence through material goods or favours, gift giving and receiving may enhance business and foster a positive business climate.

The Japanese spend $10 million each year on *oseibo*, giving such traditional gifts as seaweed, cooking oil or instant coffee to bosses and others whom they wish to impress.

Around the world (during Diwali in India, Christmas in the West, early December in Japan), any legitimate reason to give a gift is an excellent opportunity to cement a business relationship and to make known your positive feelings about an employee, client or customer.

However, it may be a good idea to have some policy regarding gift giving or receiving. Such a policy helps to prevent a conflict of interest that might compromise the integrity of the company and its employees. A major financial services institution states its policies on gifts and gratuities in this way:

Employees (including members of their immediate families) may not, directly or indirectly, take, accept or receive bonuses, fees, commissions, gifts, gratuities, excessive entertainment, or any other similar form of consideration, of other than nominal value, from any person, firm, corporation, or association with which (the institution) does or seeks to do business. Conversely, it is generally against corporate policy to give gifts or gratuities except by special approval by the General Counsel or his designee.

A conflict of interest generally does not become an issue when business gift giving involves small gifts—pens and pencils, baskets of fruit, chocolates, figurines, letter openers, Lakshmi coins, tickets to sports events or theatre, a book, picture frame, piece of clothing for a newborn child, flowers or plants, donations to charities in the name of the honoured person or providing a service such as advice.

A good way to control the possibility of abusing the positive business spirit of gift giving and receiving is to keep the cost of a gift relatively small, except for very special occasions or gifts bestowed by the highest levels of the company. The US Government allots a maximum of $25/ for a business expense for a gift, and the President of the US is restricted from accepting any gifts that cost more than $100/!!!

Another requisite of gift giving, beyond the cost of the gift, is that there be an appropriate and immediate occasion for a gift, whether it is the birth of a baby, or thanks for inviting you to a grand Diwali party. This gives a legitimate reason for the gift as well as contributes towards a definite positive feeling between you and the gift giver or receiver, so that neither will remark: 'I can't believe so-and-so sent something to me.'

Reciprocity is another important aspect of giving gifts. The fact that most people feel obliged to give in return a gift of equal value is a rule of human nature that you can use to advantage. Gift giving is therefore usually a question of keeping the scales balanced, since you get back what you give. That is why it is important to be sensitive to how you handle the gift others give you, as well as the ones that you give.

Exchanging gifts among office colleagues is fine; giving gifts to subordinates is also acceptable. In fact, some of my best neckties and cufflinks are gifts that I received from my boss at Christmas, on our wedding anniversary and on my birthday—dates he always remembered. However, giving gifts to the boss, or to a client with whom negotiations are currently on for a business deal, may be perceived as an attempt at manipulation (even though it may not be so).

Apart from all these guidelines, what is most important is the showing of care and concern, not just the value of the gift. A well-wrapped gift in appropriate gift paper (not Santa Claus print in June) with a card worded appropriately and timed with the appropriate occasion would be ideal. I received a gift for my newborn child 10 months later! And every year I spend nearly ₹200 to buy a diary in November and then receive at least 15 diaries from January to March which I have to give away. There are so many useful and appropriate gifts which are mistimed, and therefore, are wasted!

In summary, gift giving/receiving helps smoothen relationships, including business relationships, but they have to be appropriate, and correctly timed. People appreciate not just what is given, but how it is given.

46

GREATER EXPECTATIONS FROM OTHERS
IT IS FUTILE TO EXPECT GRATITUDE

A man may cause evil to others, not only by his actions but by his inaction,
and in either case he is justly accountable to them for the injury.
—JOHN STUART MILL

When we set standards for ourselves, we are inclined to think that the same standards apply to others around us. As seen earlier, values are not standard. We all know this and are convinced of it in our minds. But our emotions say something else; and we want to believe that our business associates think like we do and share the same values we cherish. This leads to greater expectations, and consequently, to greater disappointments.

There is the Biblical story of 10 lepers, who when cured, were so overjoyed that they rushed out babbling to tell the whole world about their change in fortunes, but only one went back to thank the one who had worked the cure. Just one out of the 10! This is a story that is repeated in everyone's life. While ingratitude does not surprise us, most of us are disappointed when there is an absence of even a word of thanks.

I had known Ravi for many years as an acquaintance. Two years ago he quit his job as professor in a well-known management institute and started out as a consultant. The few times I met him, I got the impression that he was finding his path steeply uphill in this new profession. My company had an assignment where we could use someone like Ravi for perhaps five days a month, for about six months. I phoned him and he readily agreed. He had been working with us as an associate for nearly a year when he began to express his unhappiness. We paid him what we had contracted. We extended the contract to 18 months from the initial agreement for six months. We helped him out when he needed both work and income. But Ravi was angry that we had not given him even more work; that we had not preferred him to other consultants on other assignments. It was not that there was not even a 'Thank you'. On the contrary, there was annoyance and resentment, because we had not met Ravi's 'greater expectations'.

Many years ago, a large group from India travelled to Singapore to attend the Asian Advertising Congress. The trip was organised by a well-known travel agency which had booked us at good hotels; arranged for local conveyance and sightseeing, and travel on airlines which were known for both punctuality and hospitality. All went well at Bangkok and Manila. But in Hong Kong we met members of another group from India who were doing a similar trip and were headed finally to the same Congress. They were staying at better hotels and we learnt that they had paid a marginally lower amount than what we had paid. Some among our group immediately drafted and circulated a memorandum for signature by all group members. This was addressed to the travel agency expressing their unhappiness with the travel arrangements and the quality of hotels. I remember Ernest Fernandes refusing to sign this, ignoring the pleas of all his companions. His argument was that our expectations had changed after meeting the other group. Before we had met them, we had been quite happy. Once again, it was greater expectations—that were making us unhappy!

It was the big exodus of the early 1970s. Two welders who were the key personnel at our factory had quit and left quite suddenly. They were headed for the Middle East for tenfold increase in income. There was a shortage of welders in Bombay. We covered every avenue and finally picked out two welders who worked at little welding outfits on Bombay's dockside for ₹300 a month, six days a week, with a 10-hour day. They joined the multinational pharmaceutical company in a Mumbai suburb, at nearly ₹1,000 per month, with an eight-hour day and a five-day week! It was three years later that there was a strike at the factory. Workers had collected at the gate to shout slogans against the general manager, the management and the company. I came out to the window to watch the goings on. Out in front, holding the banner were the two welders I had picked out, perhaps made unhappy with an income thrice as much as they were getting earlier and a work schedule one-third less rigorous. It was a case of 'greater expectations'.

George was the personnel head of a large pharmaceutical company in Mumbai and lived in my neighbourhood. He was a product of both nature and nurture. That he was from the armed forces' background and was part of a large family, gave him a natural sympathetic streak. The young, unemployed and poor from around the area targeted George for a job at the pharma plant. And most times, George was able to oblige. But he confessed to me his disappointment that only a minuscule number ever came back to say 'Thank you'. He never expected gifts; but being human like all of us, he certainly expected gratitude; and this seldom happened. He only began to have peace of mind when an elderly friend asked him one day, 'George, do you think because you have given them jobs, you have bought their minds and souls?'

Many years ago on my way from Chembur to my workplace at Ballard Estate, I used to stop at the Chembur bus stop and give a few people a lift. My only request was that there should be no conversation in the car and no smoking. Over a period of time, one gentleman seemed to have become a regular. The moment my car stopped, he would rush out of the bus queue and into the car. One day I had to receive someone at the airport in the morning and proceeded directly from the airport to my office. At 11 in the morning, Mr Rao stormed into my room in the office, furious. 'What happened to you this morning, Mr Vieira? I waited for you till 9.30 a.m. and then I had to take a taxi.' I was surprised he did not claim from me the taxi fare and some compensation for the inconvenience! It was then that I realised that every favour, over a period of time, becomes a right. Rao had developed his own 'greater expectations'. From the next day onwards, as my car passed the bus stop, Rao and others would see me deeply engrossed in reading the *Economic Times*. I gave lifts intermittently, so that a routine would not develop and expectations not raised thereby.

In many ways, managers who are trustees of wealth in Gandhian terms need to have this streak of self-abnegation. They must give without expecting in return, especially when it comes to people. An important part of a manager's job is selecting people, training them, coaching them, developing them, so that sometimes they may even go further than the one who trains them! And all this without a direct compensation. In the book *Manager Today, Executive Tomorrow*, Charles Vance highlights the point that 'no one in this entire world owes you anything', not even those closest to you.[1]

Luckily, life has a strange way of bringing about an equalisation. If we do a self-analysis, most of us will find that we have done little or nothing for those who have done a lot for us. We have perhaps not thrown even a few bits of gratitude to them, when we expect it ourselves in such ample measure!

---

[1] Vance, Charles C. 1974. *Manager Today, Executive Tomorrow*. USA: Mc Graw Hill Book Company.

47

A Yearning for Solitude
Learning to Be Alone—Not Lonely

The best thinking has been done in solitude.
The worst has been done in turmoil.
—Thomas Alva Edison

There are some who are naturally extrovert and like to be with people all the time. There are others who are naturally introvert and seek longer periods of solitude or aloneness. As they go up the executive ladder, many senior executives get into a higher stratified atmosphere and find ways to make periods of aloneness and exclusivity possible.

An industrialist buys a small island off Reunion, to be used as his exclusive and private hideout. A five-star hotel tries to negotiate with the government in the Maldives, for rights to the seaside outside the hotel to be used as a private beach, exclusively for its well-heeled clientele. The scion of a large industrial group in Mumbai hands me the key to the chairman's private toilet, for the exclusive use of the chairman and his guests. The managing director of a large multinational where I worked was never seen coming into or going out of the office. He had a private lift which brought him directly from the car park to his office. Two of the lifts at Maker Chambers in Mumbai, cannot be used by the public. These are for the private use of the owners and directors of companies in this office block. It does not matter that the other lifts are overworked! The reserved lounge at the airport is to ensure privacy for ministers and ex-ministers so that they do not have to sit with the masses whom they represent. The tycoon yearns to have his own private plane, not just for convenience but to allow personal stretch.

Someone once said to me many years ago, **'The higher you go up in life, the lonelier it gets.'** At the pinnacle of success in any field—whether in politics as prime minister or in business conglomerates as chief executive—the feeling will possibly be that of Edmund Hillary on Everest. It is the individual, not a group or a crowd. There is room for only one at the top of the pyramid. And the person who occupies this pristine position had better accept this as part of the package.

Most of these people have to choose between loneliness and aloneness. Loneliness is negative. It is morose. The person yearns for company and does not find it. He feels depressed. It is the feeling of someone who is expecting a friend, but the friend cancels the appointment. And now it is too late to make any other arrangements.

There are others who enjoy large doses of aloneness. Time to be by themselves. Time to think and to reflect. Perhaps time to plan. They enjoy their own company. They believe that **if you do not enjoy your own company, you have no business to inflict it on anyone else.**

If you do not enjoy aloneness, you run a big risk in higher positions of responsibility. You may be inclined to be over-familiar with subordinates who report to you. You may be tempted to expose confidences about persons or events. It can cause an erosion of authority of and respect for the person and the position.

People go to great lengths to protect their privacy and their personal space. Some succeed admirably. Others are not so successful. The Duke and Duchess of Windsor were quite high-profile

people, but they managed to protect their aloneness. They came
out and met the press and allowed exposure only when they chose
to or wanted to. Princess Di, on the other hand, found great dif-
ficulty in protecting her aloneness. She was constantly hounded by
photographers, whether at the gymnasium, or at the psychiatrist.

In recent times, Howard Hughes was a classic example of a
high-profile billionaire who became obsessed with the idea of protecting his aloneness. It was perhaps his insecurity and fear that
others may rob him. In fact, he went to such lengths that there was
a controversy about when he died and under what circumstances.

Stalin protected his personal space zealously and remained
alone, fearing for his life, with the knowledge that he was widely
hated. Yes, he was surrounded by guards at all times. And there
was a taster to screen out all his meals. But they were not company. He was alone—whether he enjoyed it or not is not known.
Perhaps he was lonely.

The youth hostels and YMCAs throughout the world project
the classic model of gradations in personal space. There is the low-
priced dormitory for the *hoi polloi:* beds next to each other, suitcase
under the bed, common bath and toilet facilities where you queue
up and wait your turn.

Those who value greater privacy and an opportunity for greater
aloneness, and who can afford to pay more, look for private rooms
than a dormitory. These rooms may offer privacy but the toilets
and bathrooms are shared. And those who value even greater privacy look for private rooms with an attached toilet and bath.

Those higher up the corporate or social ladder will certainly not
look at the possibility of staying in a youth hostel. They will not
even accept a single room with an attached bath. They will perhaps
want a suite which has a sitting room and a dining room, so that
they do not rub shoulders with the common folk in the hotel dining room.

My friend Sharu once met a leading architect from South
America. He asked the architect what was the most unusual
building he had designed. He thought awhile and told Sharu that
he had designed a 500-room beach resort in Venezuela with every
room having its own swimming pool. Sharu asked him whether

this made any sense. Surely it made more sense to have even four swimming pools for the general use of all residents (in case one swimming pool got too crowded) rather than a pool in each room. 'No, no, you don't understand', the architect said. 'This is a hotel for the very rich. And the richer they are, the more zealously they guard their privacy and personal space. They want to be alone. They enjoy aloneness. They don't want to be part of a crowd, even if it is of equals, unless the group is of their choosing.' For me, this story struck a chord. **Generally, the richer you get and the higher you go up the hierarchy, the greater the temptation to pull out from the crowd and be either alone or with a small group of one's choosing.**

My friend Shyam and his wife used to meet us often—generally on weekends—over many years. Either they would visit us, or we would visit them, or we would plan some outings together. Over a period of time, Shyam rose from being a junior manager to an executive director of the company. He acquired a seaside cottage at Marve. And that's where he went every Saturday evening to return on Monday morning. We no longer saw him except a few times a year. He missed many of the dinners or parties that were planned by friends for the weekend. He had withdrawn himself from the circle of friends and colleagues into the privacy of his seaside cottage and the luxury of his aloneness.

Remember the 9 Ltd BEST bus from Ghatkopar (a distant suburb) to Flora Fountain in Mumbai? This is known as the share broker special. The share brokers have been travelling together like this for years. Each one has a regular seat and they have placed themselves in groups so they can play cards on the way, with the scores spilling over to the next day and monthly accounts maintained of winnings and losses. I asked Dalal, who had now become a millionaire, whether he should not now graduate to a chauffeur-driven car. Dalal was the exception to the rule. He had 'arrived'. But he did not want to increase his privacy and personal space. He continued to enjoy the camaraderie and did not want to give this up for a lonely ride into town. Perhaps, he also benefited by the bits of share market conversation which he would have missed if he travelled alone!

But those like Dalal are different. For the rest of us who may have made it and want to pull out totally from the chaos of the 'madding crowd' to havens of 'aloneness', we would do well to remember the admonition of a subordinate to his boss. The boss had told him he could not see him now, because he had no time. 'Sam,' he said, 'I hope you never get too busy to meet people and start building walls around yourself!'

48

ARE YOU DOING WELL?
THE ANSWER CAN SPARK
SYMPATHY OR JEALOUSY

'Those Macedonians,' said he, 'are a rude and clownish people.
They call a spade a spade.'
—PLUTARCH: *APOTHEGMA OF GREAT COMMANDERS PHILIP*

We expect that everyone knows that the word 'progress' means different things to different people. Yet, most of us want to be abreast of everyone we know. And we certainly want to be abreast of all our peers.

When I meet friends and acquaintances at airports, on the road, or at parties, they greet me with 'Hello! Haven't seen you in a long time. How are you doing?' I respond saying, 'All is well.' There is generally a look of disappointment. It is seldom that there is a twinkle of gladness and a sharing of the joy of success. I have often wondered: what is the answer that people expect?

Arjun was a stockbroker. The share market was low and so was Arjun's business and income. When Shyam met him and he asked how things were with Shyam, he expected to find consolation in someone else also having problems. It would be consoling to find that he was not the only one in the dumps. To find that there were others with similar problems. That all businesses, and not just shares, were in dire straits. This would give Arjun a certain sense of fellowship, of companionship, of being comrades in arms, fighting a common war against a common enemy. When Shyam told Arjun that 'business was so-so and could be much better', Arjun's face brightened. He had found a kindred soul. He went on to tell Shyam about the problems in the share market and the share business, and how, in spite of all this, he, Arjun, had managed to keep his head above water, when some of the others had sunk.

So when someone asks, 'How are you doing?' it could be that he wants to find someone who is doing as badly or, perhaps, worse. It will then make him feel good.

There are the two different streams in the corporate world—Rajan is self-employed (the entrepreneur) and Raju is a corporate executive. Each one has the nagging and persisting feeling of self-doubt, that the grass is greener on the other side. Invariably, when self-employed Rajan asks Raju (or vice versa), 'How are things?' Rajan feels happy when the response is 'Oh, just all right. There are a lot of problems at the moment.' Surely there must be. The entrepreneur probably has problems of working capital and the corporate executive has problems getting on with his boss. So they are really telling the truth and each probably feels happy that the grass is *not* greener on the other side, after all. In fact, the more brown he sees in it, the less envious he feels.

There are those like Raman who work in family-managed companies and others like Nikhil, who work in what are euphemistically called 'professionally managed' companies. Each one looks at the other with a certain envy. Those in the family-managed company have the advantage of a paternalistic manage-ment, where they will be looked after through joys and sorrows, through marriages and major illnesses. They may not be as hand-somely paid as their confreres in professionally managed com-panies, but they are 'part of the family'. Those like Nikhil, in professionally managed companies, have the advantage of not having to kowtow to the owner (because there is none). Never mind that some professional managers act as if they own the company! A response of 'extremely well' to the usual question of

'How are you doing?' from any one to the other will only make the other unhappy and envious.

And there are those, a growing tribe, who come back to India or are recruited by the giant transnationals at gigantic salaries. They are a breed apart and constitute another focus, directly opposite to the focus provided by the local corporate executives, whether in family-owned or professionally managed corporations. They are in the 'business class' and a source of envy for those who are still in the 'economy class'. The latter like to believe that MNC executive has to work himself to the bone, for long hours and with total job insecurity for the extra money that he/she is paid. And when they are asked, 'How are you doing?' it is comforting to hear, 'It is just all right—lot of work with many deadlines to keep'. The person asking is then pleased that life for even these chosen ones is not a bed of roses. That they too have their share of thorns.

Most people we meet want to feel better because they know that others are in as bad a situation, if not worse, as they themselves. It gives them consolation that they are not the only ones to have major problems and worries. That many others—or at least most of their friends and acquaintances—have as much or more to worry about.

There are exceptions, of course. There is a small number of people who exult and are joyous over the success of their acquaintances. They do not wish that their own sorrow be transferred or distributed equitably among all those they know and even those they don't. These are people who are not petty; in fact, they are large hearted, generous and wish others well.

And there are situations such as Jack Welch taking over as CEO of General Electric (GE), at a time when the company was grovelling and bleeding. 'Poor man,' they said shaking their heads mournfully. 'I wonder why he took this. Perhaps the money tempted him. Because he will not be able to change this behemoth. He will sink with GE!' All of us know that Welch proved all his detractors wrong. He converted GE in just four years of taking over into the darling of Wall Street. Welch, therefore, was untouched by envy, and got a chance to be far ahead of the madding crowd.

Envy and jealousy kill all those who spout it, more than damaging those at the receiving end. If you believe that we are all products of nature and nurture—and destined to live and die in our own special way—the gnawing of envy at our vitals can be considerably reduced.

There is merit in the old Punjabi custom which I learnt the first time when Suri, the company's Area Manager in Punjab, constructed a beautiful new house in Amritsar in 1971. 'Mr Vieira,' he said, 'Congratulations, you have a new house.' 'Do I?' I asked, surprised. 'Yes,' he said, 'I have just completed the construction of a four-bedroom house in Amritsar. It is yours. Please feel free to come and be our guest any time you choose!' He had shared his good fortune and his joy. After such an open invitation and a well-meant one, no one could be envious of Suri!

49

FOOLING PEOPLE AT WORK
SOME OF THE PEOPLE, SOME OF THE TIME

To dream of the person you would like to be, is to waste the person you are.
—ANONYMOUS

If you have not set values and a design for the kind of life you wish to lead in the corporate world and outside it, then you can end up having very flexible standards. This can even mean 'no standards' at all. As you go up the executive ladder, keep looking around you at the people who have different standards and values.

With some of them, you will be able to quickly 'shred the veil' and identify the real person. There may be others who are more adept and are able to 'fool you' and others. I have come across many from both categories. But we cannot allow them to make us pessimists. We must opt to choose optimism instead of pessimism.

The medical director's secretary was Mr Smith—a fine, kindly man coming close to his retirement age. He had worked in the company for 27 years and was referred to as one of the 'old timers'. Unfortunately, the medical director did not have much work and Smith really had enough typing for only two hours a day. Yet, he did not want to give the impression that he was idle. So everyone in the office found Smith busy the whole day—adjusting the paper on the roller, readjusting it, then readjusting it once again. When enough was really enough, he began typing recipes from *Femina* and *Eve's Weekly*. And when he was finished with that, he just typed whatever was on the next page and the page after. It did not matter if the page said 'continued from'. All that mattered was that Smith kept typing—and everyone saw he was 'gainfully employed'. He kept his secret for many years and succeeded in fooling most of the people most of the time.

Suri, the junior officer in the Law Board (LB) office seemed very hardworking. It seemed so strange to see someone working with such zeal and dedication in a government office, where official business only began at 10 a.m. and closed at 5.30 p.m. Many employees strolled in by 10.30 a.m. and rushed out by 5.15 p.m. But Suri was different. He came in at 9.30 a.m. and generally left between 6.30 and 7 p.m. He was jeered at by other officials who did not appreciate the example he was setting. He seemed to be setting the wrong example for a government servant.

Few admired him, nodding wisely and admitting that 'this boy will go far'. The others just wondered—'What makes Suri tick? What are his ambitions?' No one really knew that Suri had a printing press. He ran the press from the LB office. He came early and made his phone calls; he tried to find prospects from among the many people who came to the LB to solve their problems; he spent the afternoon doing his press accounts; and he wound up for the day with some more calls to finish unfinished business. It was a good arrangement for Suri. It was even better that no one really knew his secret agenda and hidden motives.

Sitting late at the office was a favourite ploy in the organisation where I worked. The CEO had no other interests. He played no games, was not interested in music, had few friends, read an occasional novel, was a teetotaller and seemed not to like to even go home! He was a workaholic and sat in the office from nine to nine, putting on weight himself. And the CEO imposed his value systems on everyone else. If he found the lights in the marketing manager's cabin still on when he left for the day, then the marketing manager was perceived as good and hardworking. This was the yardstick for everyone—how late they sat in the office, how early they came in; not how much work they put in and how effective they were in their jobs. Managers competed with one another at a 'sitting' game. Sitting late in the office became part of the corporate culture.

There is a big demand for casual wear or more appropriately leisure wear these days and part of the demand is created by executives who need good leisure wear to attend the office on Saturday. In some corporations, the five-day week exists only on paper. All managers are expected to be in the office on Saturday. If someone absents himself to go out of town with his family on a long weekend it is not looked on very kindly. The corporation comes first, the family next. What is actually done on Saturday mornings is a different matter. Everyone waits to be called by the higher-ups. Some may not be called. Greater the pity. And then it is time for lunch and the freedom of the weekend, or what is left of it. But at least, he has fooled some of the people some of the time!

'He's in a meeting' the secretary tells you sweetly. 'He can't be disturbed. It is a long meeting.' This corporate manager seemed to have meetings after lunch on a daily basis, until I realised that it was really his scheduled time for a short siesta. It was the old story of 'before lunch, his mind is irritable, and after lunch, his stomach is irritable'. He got into the work system again only after the 3.30 p.m. cup of tea. And all the time, everyone thought the poor man was going through a gruelling meeting, while he relaxed in his deep executive chair, mercifully without a snore! Another ploy to fool most of the people some of the time.

And do not miss the bulging briefcase of the seemingly busy manager. To project an image of 'I'm a simple man', this senior manager will carry a salesman's bag. On the other hand, salesmen in the company keep hankering for executive briefcases from VIP because they do not want to appear in the marketplace as 'just salesmen'. The bulging briefcase contains an odd collection of old issues of *BusinessWorld, Economic Times, Harvard Business Review* and assorted files. The bag goes home and comes back unopened, then goes home again. Everyone around is suitably impressed— the boss, colleagues and staff, except if some of them are adopting the same technique themselves. The bulging briefcase does help to fool most of the people at least some of the time.

It is often said that you cannot fool all the people all the time and this may well be true. However, in the corporate world, you can manage to fool some of the people some of the time or, even, a lot of the time. The 'busy' look, coming early and staying late, the casual Saturday morning appearance, and the bulging briefcase are proven and time-tested techniques for achieving this goal!

50

WITH A LITTLE BIT OF LUCK FORTUNES CAN CHANGE!

This is courage ... to bear unflinchingly what Heaven sends.

—*EURIPIDES*

It is one of those things. In the rough and tumble of corporate politics, many things can happen. Some will suffer for no fault of their own. Others will be plummeted to the top or towards it, with little contribution of their own. Sparks emanate from red hot cinders and depending on where they fall, some will help to light new fires; others will fall and die out.

Most of us would have read and mulled over Shakespeare's quote:

There is a tide in the affairs of men,
Which, taken at the flood, leads on to fortune;
Omitted, all the voyage of their life
Is bound in shallows, and in miseries.

My friend Rajan worked as a salesman in a music shop. A very presentable young man, he spoke very well and had a pleasing, attractive personality. He had completed Inter Arts, got involved with an amateur jazz combo and given up further studies, much to the disappointment of his parents. He had worked as a music shop salesman for two years when the chairman of a large multinational company came in to buy some records; became very impressed with Rajan's salesmanship qualities, gave Rajan his visiting card and told him to drop by and see him if he ever thought of taking up another assignment. Rajan took him up on his offer and met him the next week. He joined the ANZ Company as a trainee. Exactly 12 years later, Rajan was appointed the regional manager for South Asia for the Agro Products Division at the World Corporate Headquarters in New York. Rajan had gone a long way from the music shop in downtown Bombay to downtown New York, because with good luck, he got a break, worked hard and never looked back. Lady Luck had smiled on him.

Paul had been the head of a large advertising agency which was plagued with staff union problems. The agency services deteriorated; began losing clients with predictability, the blue chip ones going first; and finally it was Paul's turn to go. He had no choice but to quit. The pressures that built up round him were too many to manage. And he could not buy time to first find another assignment and then resign. A fortnight after he had quit, he was flying to Delhi to tie up some loose ends, when he met Kimani, an industrialist from Hong Kong. Kimani was in the next seat and after the plane took off, they struck up a conversation. Kimani got to like Paul; asked whether Paul would be interested in a general manager's position in Hong Kong with one of Kimani's companies; and fixed the time and place for the next meeting. Two months later, Paul was installed in his new assignment in Hong Kong. He has now been there for 14 years and has since become the managing director of the company. Lady Luck had smiled on him.

There was the nondescript accounts clerk Ravi who—by the use of a judicious balance of hard work and total allegiance to his boss, and by maintaining a distance from corporate politics and projecting himself as a 'non-threat' to everyone in the organisation—rose to be the managing director. He moved first to accounts executive, then finance manager and then finance controller. The managing director, who was earlier finance director, died suddenly of a heart attack. The marketing director took his place, and on becoming managing director threw a sop and elevated the finance controller to finance director. After four years, the managing director took an assignment abroad with the same company. He needed someone who would be a figurehead managing director and not challenge his own authority. He chose the finance director as his successor. Ravi had neither the intelligence, the force of character, the imagination, nor the vision to be the CEO. He was, therefore, happy that not much was expected from him except to be 'his master's voice'. He was also happy with his undeserved status and all the trimmings that went with it. So he went through the five-year term—an uneventful period both for himself and the company. Lady Luck had been kind to him. He had come a long way—from accounts clerk to managing director, something he would never have believed in his wildest dreams. But deaths and transfers and his own stodginess of mind and heart had helped to make a dream come true!

Most companies will not re-employ a manager who has left their services. But Shah, who was with the Angus Corporation for 18 years, had risen from sales assistant to sales manager, left to join Seagull Corporation as marketing manager, found he had made the wrong choice and was re-employed by Khanna, a mediocre, weak-kneed MD of Angus, as general manager, marketing. Shah returned in glory—with much greater 'appreciation' as reflected in his salary and perquisites as compared to only two years ago. And he pushed the advantage through. But Shah was knowledgeable and a good worker. He contributed to the company, as good as they gave him. Yet, he never knew what Lady Luck had in store for him. Six months later, Khanna developed an incurable and galloping cancer and died. Shah was installed as the new managing director. Lady Luck had smiled on him—again and yet again. It was unexpected and welcome. He was the right man, in the right place, at the right time.

What happens when Lady Luck frowns? That can happen as unexpectedly and as suddenly as when she smiles. Mohan graduated from Cambridge University and was selected in 1958 as a management trainee for the Indian affiliate of a large UK-based multinational. He worked there for eight years and was the sales promotion executive when he resigned. His father was the major shareholder of a medium-sized but well-known food product company and often requested Mohan (his only child) to come and join the family business which was founded by Mohan's grandfather. 'It is a shame,' Mohan's father confided to close friends, 'that Mohan should waste his talents being a small cog in a large multinational, when he has the better alternative of building up his own business.' Mohan finally relented and joined the family business as deputy managing director. All went well until three years later, someone who had been cornering the company's stock in the market came in and announced that he had become the major shareholder in the company. Unknown to the family, they had lost ownership control of the company. Mohan's father quit first as managing director. Mohan had to follow suit some months later. He was now 40 years old. Having been deputy managing director, he found it difficult to find an equivalent level job. He got frustrated and took to drink. He kept blaming his father for having dragged him from the multinational, where he had established himself and was happy. He kept looking at the past, never at the future, and his life was in ruins. Lady Luck had frowned!

It is necessary to do one's best and follow all the principles in the book. But it is not possible to run life on a tight leash. If Lady Luck smiles, the executive path is strewn with roses. If she frowns, it is the thorns which will hurt even covered feet.

51

Values and the Executive
Some Things Are Unchangeable, Even in a Changing World

The time is always right to do what is right.
—*Rev. Martin Luther King Jr.*

I have come across so much scepticism whenever I discuss executive life and basic values, that I am reminded of the story of the preacher who ended his sermon with 'Remember, my brothers and sisters, there is no buying and selling in heaven.' A bored executive on one of the last pews got so fed up that he yelled back, 'That's not where business has gone anyway.'

Yes, 'business has gone to hell' is the refrain heard from executives everywhere. But we cannot sit back and passively accept this state of affairs. We need to do something about it. And the best summary that I have come across is the one put forward by Vance in his book *Manager Today, Executive Tomorrow.*[1]

---

[1] Vance, Charles C. 1974. *Manager Today, Executive Tomorrow.* USA: Mc Graw Hill Book Company.

Vance gives eight basic attitudes. These are:

(1) From birth to death we are alone.

There is no one in the entire world who can help us or be with us all the time. One's parents are there through infancy, childhood and perhaps a part of adulthood. One may have brothers and sisters and friends. They will all be with you some of the time through the course of your life.

And again, your spouse and children will be with you part of the time. But the permanent company you will keep is yourself. Because from birth to death, you are alone, only interspersed with periods of togetherness.

That is why you have to learn to enjoy your own company, to convert the concept of 'loneliness' to a concept of 'aloneness'. Loneliness is negative, depressing, sorrowful, stark. Aloneness is positive, enjoyable, rejuvenating.

There seems to be a lot of sense in this guideline. It makes you less dependent on other people, on the movies, TV programmes or the video films. It is important to face up to the reality that from birth to death you are alone, and adopt a positive attitude towards this inescapable truth.

(2) No one in this entire world owes you anything.

This is a very difficult attitude to adopt because we are all brought up to believe that everyone should do things for us. We all have expectations, some very high, and some totally divorced from reality. This is because we do not understand and accept the positive success-generating attitude that 'no one you meet in your entire life owes you anything'.

If anything is given to you, it should be graciously accepted. If it is denied to you, it is pointless being annoyed. There are no rights or favours that are done for you.

Much of the unhappiness in the world today is not because people have less than in the earlier generation. It is because expectations have changed and increased, and when these expectations are not met, people get annoyed and revolt.

(3) The word 'Progress' means different things to different people.

Most people measure their own progress based on where they stand in relation to those friends who have perhaps gone places and are apparently very successful. So, because my friend who graduated with me 25 years ago is now an assistant director with World Bank in Washington, I am unhappy. Because another friend of mine is now a cardiologist in London, practises at Harley Street and stays in a large five-bedroom mansion near London, I feel unhappy.

This is because I am measuring my own progress by the achievements of others. Vance suggests that we measure progress by the objectives we have set ourselves in life, and how far we have achieved these objectives. It's like the basic rule followed in athletics and racing: 'Always look forward. Keep your eyes on the finishing line. If you look back to see where the others are, you may slip up in that brief moment and lose the race.' Never mind about what other people are doing or have done. Let them do their own thing, as you are doing yours. Let them follow their own star, while you follow yours. Because progress means different things to different people.

(4) In life, accept that you are going to win some, lose some.

Some people get so spoilt as children because their parents give them everything they ask for, from ice-cream to clothes to expensive toys. Later, they cannot face a situation where they cannot get everything they want. They do not realise that life is like a one-day cricket match and only one side can win; sometimes you win, sometimes you lose.

The really complete person faces up to failure with some disappointment, but without the depression bordering on wanting to commit suicide. Because he knows that in life 'You win some, and you lose some. You don't win all the time.'

(5) A life without problems is impossible.

Most of us are looking for an ideal life, where we will encounter total happiness and contentment without any clouds of sorrow. But this is a dream. It never happens. Perhaps it happens in novels, in unrealistic movies and in short stories. But not in real life.

Life is always a graph of high and low points, of peaks and valleys. Some may have longer periods of peaks and smaller intervals of valleys. For others it may be the other way round. But we all have our due share of both, whether we are born rich or poor, intelligent or dull, handsome or ugly, brown or white.

(6) No matter what others say, you never stop learning.

There will be the pessimists and cynics who keep telling you that the world is a cruel place. That merit really gets you nowhere. That everywhere it is now a question of how you can buy your way through with either money or influence, or both. That the boss goes by how many favours you have done for him rather than by how well you have done your work.

There are others who will tell you that there is nothing new in the world. That you can't teach an old dog new tricks. That all supposedly new knowledge is 'old wine in new bottles'. But the world is changing so fast. Technology is being updated every day, not just every year. New concepts are being put forward and old theories disproved. It is a fast-changing world. At least 70 per cent of the products you buy today were not available 50 years ago. Unless you keep learning and keep abreast of what is going on, both in your own field as well as in the general environment, you will be outdated and soon become obsolete.

(7) Change is taking place all the time and you must welcome it.

Most people don't. They prefer the familiar, standard routine with everything in its place. People don't like to change their homes to bigger houses and better surroundings because of the fear of the unfamiliar. It is only the positively oriented who welcome change and enjoy it. They do not wait for everyone else to change and then join them. They are amongst the first. They are 'the change agents'.

They realise that 'the only permanent feature of life is change'.

Change also involves learning or relearning, which most people resent. But the change agent does not resent it in spite of the trouble it involves. He understands and accepts the fact that he must welcome change.

(8) You must choose optimism instead of pessimism.

It is so easy these days to be pessimistic. The examination papers are leaked out and sold. There is cheating at the exams. You can't get admission into professional colleges even with 90 per cent marks. Jobs are only obtained by influence. Fast progress in one's career needs a godfather. The country is going to pieces. There is corruption everywhere. The old sense of ethical values has totally vanished. The price of necessities is spiralling!

All this is enough to depress any normal human being. But it can't be allowed to happen. As Henry Thoreau said, 'Men were born to succeed, not to fail.' A person with a positive attitude looks at the bright side of things and moves forward. He looks for ways and means to bring about changes and improve the environment. Instead of being totally influenced by others, he makes an effort to influence others. All the time he asks himself, 'What can I do about it?'

Eight basic values, which can help the executive to go through life as a 'living' human being, instead of being a zombie!

52

SHOULD YOU BE IN BUSINESS?
WITH THE RIGHT NATURE AND
NURTURE, YOU SHOULD

'I wish I were in business' is a refrain often heard in India. It is the favourite of many corporate executives—from managing directors to junior product executives. There are some good reasons for this.

One is the taxation structure. The time, effort and sacrifices made to climb the corporate ladder, seem to be too high a price to pay for the monetary rewards that are finally gained as 'after tax' salary and perquisites. Besides the trimmings of a stylish office, an attractive secretary and a credit card for entertaining, there would seem to be little left to be set aside for a rainy day.

The second is the galloping rate of inflation. The large provident fund and gratuity and even the insurance money, may be worth little in purchasing power when one has finally retired. It may seem to be a huge sum of money, but one may not be able to maintain any reasonable standard of living after retirement, if one has not invested savings wisely.

The third factor is that corporate executives believe that all those in business are well off. This is because the executive generally meets only the successful businessman, whether socially or professionally. The failures fall by the wayside. They are not in circulation, and are therefore seldom seen. This can lead one to the false assumption that all those who go into business are successful. This is obviously not so.

But should the successful corporate executive move out and go into business? Should he succumb to temptation, and the inner voice that seems to prod him every time he meets a person who is happily on his own? Should he take the plunge into the unknown, where he can flex his muscles, and not be fettered by corporate organisational chains? Should he begin now, and build up a business in the manner in which he always felt a business should be built; and which, finally, he can leave for his children? The answers will depend on the responses that he gives to some of the questions asked below:

(1) Do you have the ability to take risks? Personal risks?

Sure, these will be calculated risks, not just venturing into the unknown without proper homework. But they are risks nonetheless. A corporate executive could have the ability to take a decision to risk ₹50 million on a new project; but he may not have the ability to risk ₹10,000 of his own money on a small venture. The dimension of risk taking changes—surprising but true. This does not have anything to do with having money or not having it. In fact, there are many who have been paupers—and who have borrowed money and gone into business. Money is not the critical element, risk-taking ability is. Perhaps a person cannot be trained in risk taking. It is a natural ability. You are either born with it; or not born with it. If you are not, it is better to remain content under the secure umbrella of the corporation.

(2) Do you have the intense faith in yourself; in your own abilities?

It is faith that sustains a person. Because when you go into business, most of your relatives and friends and business associates will dissuade you. Perhaps even your own wife and parents will throw cold water on your proposed plan of action. When you have already gone into business, many of your supposed well wishers will try and ensure that you do not succeed. Once you are successful, all of them will fawn on you. But before that, there will be attitudes ranging from envy and jealousy to downright malice all cloaked with 'sympathy' for the 'poor chap'.

It is not easy to fight these battles on so many fronts unless you have intense faith in yourself and in your own abilities. It is a kind of religious fervor, a total sense of dedication and commitment. It may not be perceptible on the surface—but it burns inside, nevertheless. It is the kind of commitment which made a Hussain rise from a poster painter to a world renowned artist; a Godrej from a cycle repairer to a formidable industrialist. If you don't have this inner faith—stay in your job. It is safer than being exposed to a multitude of Doubting Thomas and then beginning to doubt yourself.

(3) Do you have the ability to persevere?

In personal business life, especially in the initial stages there can be many ups and downs. One has to take the downs with as much equanimity as the ups. You cannot close shop and go away. You have to steer the ship though rough weather and stormy seas. Perhaps you may amend your course, but generally you will want to go in the predetermined direction.

As a corporate executive, the ups and downs of the organisation did matter to you; you were concerned; and you took action to remedy the situation to the extent possible within your authority and responsibility. But you got your pay cheque at the end of the month. Where it came from did not bother you. As a businessman you will have to ensure that your employees are paid *their* cheques. In the process you may have to go hungry yourself. But *you are* the company—even if you are the promoter of a limited company. It revolves round you. It is a tremendous responsibility. And therefore there is no place for fickleness of mind and inconstancy of purpose. It requires the ability to persevere.

It needs the ability to be a *doer, thinker and integrator*.

Every management team must have a balance of 'producers' who are practical doers and followers of instructions; of 'processors' who are the thinkers, who are planning and creative people; and the small minority of people who generally make it to the top of the organisation ladder, who are 'integrators' and who orchestrate the activities of both doers and thinkers to achieve the company's set objectives.

In a large organisation there is enough elbow room for all three categories. One can belong to any category and be quite successful. You may not reach the top if you are not an integrator—but you could come close to it.

When you get into business you have to be a doer, a thinker, as well as an integrator. You cannot afford to have a large staff with a balance of all three types. You have to plan, implement and follow up, yourself. You will have to obtain forms yourself, fill them in and apply for licences (like sales tax registration); go to meet minor officials, stand in queues waiting for them, and be spoken to with superciliousness by minor officials. They will call you again and again until you are exasperated with the whole system. And you have to accept this with patience and an outward smile. If you can't and you feel like throwing in the towel and quitting; if you do not have the doggedness to persevere—then don't even begin. Business is not for you!

(4) Do you have the ability to change your living standards?

When you move from being a corporate executive to a private businessman, there are many changes that will be required in your living standards. You will have to live frugally at least in the initial stages; you may now have to travel by bus and not in a chauffer-driven car, live in a smaller apartment, in a more distant suburb, travel outstation by bus or train and not by air; and stay at small, economy hotels. The five star treatment must remain a pleasant memory. There will no longer be trips to conferences abroad; no leave travel allowances which can take you and your family to Kashmir or Goa, perhaps even no leave at all. The visits to the club will have to be less frequent. There will probably be no time to visit the club anyway, because you will have to work long hours. All this can be hard on you—but it can be harder on the family. If you are not certain that you can take irregular hours—or that your family will accept this disturbance in their social routine, then don't try your own business. It's not for you.

There are a number of executives who will say that if they can somehow maintain present living standards, they would go into business without a second thought. This is a dream. There has to be a trough before a crest. And sometimes the trough may be deep enough and over a period long enough to test the mettle of any corporate executive. There can never be a transition so smooth that the executive and his family will not feel the difference.

(5) Do you have the ability to be wealthy and yet remain humble?

As corporate executives most people become slightly overbearing personalities, the more so the higher they rise up the executive ladder. The bigger you are, the more people report to you, directly or indirectly, more people flatter you, listen to you attentively, run around doing small favours for you. All heads turn towards the door when you enter the conference room; people move aside to let you pass along the office corridor. All this feeds the executive ego and the corporate executive begins to believe that this is right. It would be wrong if this did not happen. In fact, after retirement, it is this that executives miss, more than the money they would have got on the job. But the businessman's attitude is different. Look at the company stockist and suppliers who come to your office. They are probably wealthier than many corporate executives. But they don't wear their riches on their sleeves. They are quite humble, soft spoken, careful. It is an attitude of mind which has to be developed. It is the other end of the spectrum from the normal attitudes of corporate executives. And if this cannot be developed, then it is better not to get into business. If you do, you will not remain there very long.

Corporate executives may keep talking about getting into business; about the frustrations of working in the corporate sector; about the freedom they need to fly the open skies; to test and experiment with their novel ideas; to introduce new products and strike new paths in a growing and developing country like India. They complain about the inadequacy of the compensation after taxes; about not getting on with their bosses; and they will say that they would have certainly gone into business on their own, if they had sufficient financial backing; if they owned their own house rather than staying in a company apartment; if they owned their own car; if their wives would accept the idea of moving to a distant suburb or another town.

In the final analysis, it is not the talking or the excuses, but the five criteria given above which will determine whether the corporate executive will start his own business or not.

53

CHARACTER AND SELF DISCIPLINE
THE FOUNDATION FOR LEADERSHIP

Francis Bacon started his famous essay on Truth with 'What is truth? said Pontius Pilate, and would not wait for an answer.'

I sit here and read about Harshad Mehta, who became a hero to the young generation and was author of the biggest stock market scam in India. A boy from a small town with little education and no money, or connections; who became the undisputed 'king' of the stock market. He was finally 'found out', and convicted—but died before this happened, so he did not spend time in jail.

I read about Ketan Parekh who followed in the footsteps of Harshad, some years later. He was smarter, kept a low profile, did not attempt to achieve film star status the way Harshad did. But was also finally found out and convicted. There were banks that failed because of Ketan. Many thousands lost their life's savings and were ruined. Ketan was out on bail and barred from trading on the stock exchange. Rumour has it that he traded anyway under 'benami' or 'front' names. And the show goes on.

And then we have the 'mother of all scams'—the great Satyam circus of Ramalinga Raju. The man who was elected 'Entrepreneur of the Year' by Ernst and Young the famed international management consulting company. He appeared on TV in London at the award ceremony and looked so 'smart' in a butterfly collar and bow tie and gave a nice speech to explain how he did it, and how young people could now also follow his example. Little did we know, as we watched, that concurrently as he spoke, he was also milking the company and would finally end with a ₹7000 crore scam, among the biggest in India's corporate history!

I was in Singapore some time ago and took a public taxi from my hotel to the airport. On arrival at the airport, the meter showed $24. He gave me $9 back against the $30 I gave him. "Hello—that's wrong. You need to give me just $6". 'No,' he said 'I took a longer route, because part of the regular route is under repairs. No need for you to pay for this longer route.' 'Then keep this as a tip' I said. The response was prompt. 'We do not accept tips in Singapore Sir. Thank you very much.'

Many years ago, I read that a good conscience is what impels you to do right, when no one is looking. And you had the opportunity to have done wrong and could have got away with it. It is like driving through the red light because it is 11 at night, and there is no cop at the crossing.

The taxi driver in Singapore, met this criterion admirably. A simple man of average means, doing a routine job—but a man of 'character'. The millionaires like Harshad, Ketan and Ramalinga are at the other 'black end' of the spectrum. They are millionaires without character.

And what is the foundation of Character? It is Discipline. Not the kind of discipline that is served out in schools or in homes; but self-discipline. Something that you choose to do and do. Which then makes you a better person. An exemplary person.

Aristotle had said that 'I count him brave who overcomes his desires than him who conquers his enemies; for the hardest victory is over self.' Discipline helps to overcome the changes people encounter in their journey to progress. It helps to deal with disappointments, which will inevitably take place.

When I see old people walk pass my house at 5.30 or 6.00 a.m. in the morning—going for their one-hour morning walk; when I see young students running to the Club at 6 a.m. for tennis practice; when I see people go every Wednesday for prayer devotions to Mahim in Mumbai year after year, I think of discipline. They belong to a minority of people who have persistence—lack of which is a common weakness with a majority of people.

I was greatly influenced during my days in college, with the example of a senior who I hardly knew. He was a friend of friends. But he had set his mind on joining the IFS. After he did his Masters, he spent a whole year preparing for the exams. He refused to attend any parties. Did not go to movies. His only recreation was a walk down the Oval Maidan in the evenings. He refused to be distracted. And when the results were out, Sinai had stood first both at the IAS and IFS. It was not just intelligence, but a large dollop of discipline added to intelligence, which had brought him to the top of the heap.

Sinai had followed four simple but necessary steps to develop discipline:

(1) Have a clearly defined goal
(2) Have a definite plan of action to accomplish the goal
(3) Close the mind to all negative influences
(4) Find a mentor who will hold you accountable

As you develop your 'discipline'—it becomes easier to feel more confident and stronger in character. Self-discipline is an act of cultivation. It requires you to connect today's actions to tomorrow's results. It's not easy to say No to destructive feelings, uncontrolled cravings and selfish desires.

54

The Protective Umbrella
For Many, the Grass Is
Greener Here

God doesn't make orange juice; God makes oranges.
—Jesse Jackson, *Civil Rights Leader*

People working in the corporate world repeatedly talk about how much better it is to be 'on one's own'—where they can do what they like and be totally independent; where they can freely implement their innovative ideas and not kowtow to the boss; where they are not constrained by the parameters set by company policy; where they do not have to meekly accept the annual performance evaluation; where they get a low increment totally disproportionate to the contribution that they have made; where 'location transfers' create havoc with family and career plans; where politics becomes more important than achieving corporate objectives and where, however, well one may perform as an individual, if the whole company is doing poorly, one has to also pay the price for no fault of one's own. So much for the trials and tribulations of being an employee or even a manager or an executive director in the corporate world!

Some of those who feel this way may well be able to strike out on their own and become 'entrepreneurs'. There may be a few, who have the good fortune to work for a company where they can evolve into 'intrapreneurs'. There will be those who take matters into their hands and, quite unethically, become 'extrapreneurs'. But the numbers who can graduate into any of these categories are small. The large majority are fated to continue in the corporate world—and would be wiser to accept this, look at the positives and enjoy it while it lasts.

And what are the positives of working in the corporate world? There are many but in our anxiety to see the grass on the other side, most of us ignore the freshly mowed lawn under our own feet. There is the oft-quoted story of two salesmen who were sent by competitive shoe companies to a country in Africa. Two days after they arrived, one sent a cable to his head office in Europe that said, 'Returning home tomorrow. No scope for sales of shoes. Nobody wears shoes here.' The other salesman sent a cable to his head office saying, 'Staying one month. Send 1,000 pairs urgently. Great potential. Nobody wears shoes here.' The same market situation, the same product and the same country. And yet, the two different attitudes make the difference.

Those who choose to stay in the corporate world and spend a lifetime there, because they lack 'what it takes' to be in business on their own, would benefit by making life more pleasant and enjoyable for themselves, their families and everyone around them. Light a candle, rather than curse the darkness. Stop complaining that you have no shoes, there are those who have no feet!

Remember that in the corporate world, you **are 'pre-sold' as an individual**, by the reputation and image of your company. The aura of the company encompasses all those who work in it. 'Mr Shah of ABB' or 'Mr Atul of Siemens', they will whisper. The weight of the big name will add weight to the employee's. The person immediately gets an identity.

On one's own, one will have to build one's identity and that can take a long, long time. The company provides a 'spillover' effect and the bigger the company, the greater is the 'spillover'.

In the corporate world, you have the comfort **of being part of a group**. You are not alone. When you fly to Guwahati, the regional manager is there to receive you, a car is arranged for your transport, a hotel room is booked, the following day's work schedule all organised and the appointments already made. It is a great comfort and gives you a sense of security.

When you are on your own and have a small outfit, you arrive, look for a cab, look for a hotel and try and set up appointments. In short, you have to fend for yourself.

In the corporate world, you have **the advantage of a large infrastructure**. You take it for granted that you have facilities of a photocopier and fax machine; a computer on your desk and perhaps e-mail; of secretarial and work assistance (although it may be less than what you think you should have); of STD connections and a direct personal line and perhaps a gold credit card when travelling abroad.

On your own, all this has to be paid for. You have to generate the profit to spend on such accoutrements that you think will generate more profit. In a company, the infrastructure is immediately demanded. On your own, the infrastructure has to be slowly earned.

In the corporate world, you have the **advantage of interaction with many minds**. You can test ideas, plans and programmes with others who are your superiors, peers and subordinates. After all, good suggestions and refinements can come from any quarter, and you can interact with people both within your own function and from other functions. It is a question of many heads being better than a few (unfortunately, many in the corporate world do not appreciate the advantages that they have of being part of a team, and often try to go it alone).

When you are on your own or with a very small group, you have to largely depend on yourself or interact with those outside the orbit of your own business, i.e. friends, old colleagues, consultants and the like.

The corporate world **gives you a form of 'group insurance'**. The individual may perform poorly for some time, but the company goes on. The company has the ability to keep cruising along even with some poor performers on board and thus carries all passengers. The work and risks are shared. If advertising agencies have to be paid by the marketing division, the finance division can be expected to find the money to make the payments, even in a tight money situation. It is the same with production and purchase departments. Each one plays a role and it is an orchestra that finally produces a symphony.

The lone player or a small combo tries to play solo. At best, these days he may use a synthesiser and produce a five-piece-band music, but he carries the total load. When he stops playing, the music stops. There is no one else to handle another part of the function, to hold his hand, to cover for him to provide support.

Yes, we have come to an era of downsizing and de-layering and business re-engineering. The VRS virus can catch any of us. But on one's own, one already starts with a downsized operation. The only further downsizing possible is to close.

With so many superiors, peers and subordinates around, the corporation gives a **readymade social environment**. One meets others at games, at drinks, at dinners. Wives meet other wives and one's children meet others' children. Large establishments such as steel, cement and aluminium companies have colonies of their own. The interaction there may be even closer. At times, there may be an overdose of interaction. But it is there to partake of, nevertheless.

In your own business, such social interaction within the group is minimal. The numbers, variety and choices are missing. The kaleidoscope of group formations and reformations is not easily possible. Many try to remedy this by joining the Lions Club or such other service organisations. To an extent, they succeed. But this does not entirely substitute the easy, social intercourse of those who work against the backdrop of a common organisation.

Have you seen a cartoon of an old decrepit doctor in a wheelchair examining a patient with a stethoscope? Such individualists and those in business for themselves seldom plan to or successfully retire. Like old soldiers they fade away. Or die with their boots on. The corporation allows the individual to slowly disengage himself and plan for retirement. The larger number of people, the concept of delegation, of succession planning, of empowerment—all help to ensure a smooth transition, for both the company and the individual. Despite this facility, many corporate executives do not plan for retirement; this is entirely their own fault and a sin of omission.

The single individual or small businessman has to make a far greater effort to disengage and to plan for retirement. Most times, he finds the effort so great that he uses the ostrich technique, buries his head in the sand and ignores the reality.

To those who can and will fulfill the criteria for successful entrepreneurship—good luck! To those many others who will work under the protective umbrella of the corporation, a message—take heart, enjoy yourself and appreciate the protection from the sun and the rain!

ABOUT THE AUTHOR

Walter Vieira is the President of Marketing Advisory Services Group, which he founded in 1975. Prior to that, he spent 14 years working with various corporations—Glaxo, Warner Lambert and the Boots Company. A Certified Management Consultant and a Fellow of the Institute of Management Consultants of India, he provides training services and consultancy in business and marketing strategies to several organisations in India and abroad.

Walter Vieira has taught at leading management institutes in India, and has lectured at the J.L. Kellogg School of Management, Northwestern University, Drexel Business School, Philadelphia and Cornell Business School, all in the USA; Boston Management School, Zaragosa, Spain and many others. He was invited to address the World Congress of Management Consultants in Rome (1993), Yokohama (1996) and Berlin (1999), and has been active in social marketing for organisations such as Cancer Aid, World Wildlife Fund and Consumer Education and Research Council. Walter Vieira has served as the President of the Institute of Management Consultants of India (1987–1992), was the Founder Chairman of the Asia–Pacific Conference of Management Consultants (1989–1990) and Chairman of the International Council of Management Consulting Institutes, USA (World apex body) (1997–1999).

He has published more than 9000 articles in the business and general press and is on the Advisory Board of the *Journal of Management Consultants*, USA. Walter Vieira has also authored 11 books of which 3 were written jointly with C. Northcote Parkinson and M.K. Rustomji. His most recent books include *The New Sales Manager* and *Successful Selling*.

Walter was given the Lifetime Achievement Award for Consulting in India in 2005; and the Lifetime Achievement Award for

Marketing in India in 2009. Walter is on the world speaker list at <speakersacademy.eu> in Europe; and Philip Kotler, the world guru of Marketing describes him as one of the best speakers on Marketing in Asia.

For more on Walter Vieira, go to waltervieira.com or write to waltervieira@gmail.com

DATE DUE

PRINTED IN U.S.A.